D1420293

PESTALOZZI'S

LEONARD AND GERTRUDE

TRANSLATED AND ABRIDGED

BY

EVA CHANNING.

University Press of the Pacific
Honolulu, Hawaii

Leonard and Gertrude

by
Johann Heinrich Pestalozzi

Translated and Abridged by Eva Channing

ISBN: 1-4102-1095-2

Copyright © 2004 by University Press of the Pacific

Reprinted from the 1898 edition

University Press of the Pacific
Honolulu, Hawaii
http://www.universitypressofthepacific.com

In order to make original editions of historical works available to scholars at an economical price, this facsimile of the original edition of 1898 is reproduced from the best available copy and has been digitally enhanced to improve legibility, but the text remains unaltered to retain historical authenticity.

TRANSLATOR'S PREFACE.

———◦◊◦———

PESTALOZZI'S "Leonard and Gertrude" was first published in the year 1781 when about one fourth of the whole work appeared. Three more volumes came out in 1783, 1785 and 1787. In 1790–92 a second edition, revised and condensed by the author, appeared in three volumes. When Pestalozzi collected his works, and had them published by Cotta in Stuttgart (1819–26), he remodelled the first edition, especially the last three volumes, expanding it to such a degree that the whole work was intended to occupy six volumes. Of these, only the first four appeared, the manuscript of the fifth being lost after the author's death. Seyffarth's more modern edition, which fills five volumes, aims to hold fast to what is best in the first edition, without losing sight of the added material in the third, often calling attention in the notes to the divergence of the two.

An abridged translation of "Leonard and Gertrude" is beset with many difficulties, since the different editions vary considerably from each other, and it is impossible to hold to one of them consistently throughout. In the preparation of the present book, the only accessible material was the following : the cheap Reclam edition, comprising the first two volumes alone, and following in the main the original edition; the expanded but incomplete Cotta edition; the eclectic edition of Seyffarth in five volumes; and the latter's shortened popular version in one volume (1874), which, however, was far too prolix to serve as the basis of the present book. Vol. VII of the "American Journal of Education" (1859) contains a very literal English translation of the original first volume (a reprint of the London translation of 1824, with corrections), beside extracts from later portions of the work, regarding the school in Bonnal; these last are translated by Mr. Frederick B. Perkins, from a work by Christoffel which has extracts from the first edition. This volume of the Journal also gives a useful list of publications by and relating to Pestalozzi.

A more diffuse and tedious style than Pestalozzi's can hardly be imagined, as the reader can convince himself by turning to the London translation above mentioned. Despite the high moral tone, sound common sense, and rare insight into human character which are everywhere displayed, it is impossible to read half a dozen pages without a disposition to yawn. This circumstance, added to the unwieldy dimensions of the work, may serve as some excuse for the wholesale process of abridgment adopted in the present volume. Owing to this condensation, much of the quaint simplicity of the original has of necessity been sacrificed, although it has been retained to some degree in the dialogues. The scenes with Gertrude and her children have suffered the least mutilation of any in the book, since they are not only among the most charming, but also possess the greatest value from an educational point of view.

Externally, "Leonard and Gertrude" occupies a somewhat peculiar position in literature, since it is neither precisely a story, nor a pedagogical treatise. It might rather be called a realistic picture of Swiss peasant life in the last century, which if not of absorbing interest, yet contains much that is curious and instructive concerning old manners and customs. But the moral value of the work is far more than this. The village of Bonnal is intended to typify the world, and in describing the measures taken to reform the corruption and raise the moral standard of this little community, the author expresses his views on some of the greatest social and political questions of all ages. His opinions and theories on educational topics are scattered incidentally throughout the book, although they find their fullest expression in Chapters VIII, X, XVI, XVII, XXIII, XXV, XXXI, XXXII.

We cannot help being struck with the high esteem in which woman is held by Pestalozzi. In Gertrude he has not only painted the loving wife and mother, the charitable neighbor, and the thrifty housekeeper; but he has made her a pattern of high moral rectitude, endowed her with remarkable executive ability, and given her an intellectual clear-sightedness of a very high order. Thus it is Gertrude alone who originates the improved system of education which is afterward transferred to the Bonnal school. Furthermore, after adopting her principles, the organizers of the new school declare that the coöperation of her mother's heart is essential to insure its success, notwithstanding that the schoolmaster will bring a father's heart into his new vocation. We also find a striking tribute to the sound judgment of enlightened womanhood, in the provision made by Arner, that the commission appointed to investigate the value of the innovations in Bonnal shall include women of various classes, " who shall view the matter with their woman's eyes, and be sure that there is nothing visionary in the background."

It is hoped that the present shortened version of "Leonard and Gertrude," despite its many imperfections, may secure for this remarkable book of a remarkable man a still wider and more appreciative circle of readers than it has hitherto found.

E. C

INTRODUCTION.

THIS homely tale was not written for the modern novel-reader. It is a story of deep and ardent love, not for an individual, but for the wretched, the weak, and for children. Though he wrote much, the author could tell no tale but this. Its purpose was his earnest inner life, and its details a picture of his own surroundings, as humble and as realistically depicted as anything in Heyse or Auerbach. It is of peasants who kick their wives, of hungry children who steal a handful of raw potatoes, and who only on gala-days have the cream left on their milk; of literal dunghills and stable-drains. It is, moreover, fairly packed with incident and character. The hypocrite, the fool, the gossip, the miser, the sot, the sycophant, the schemer, the just judge, the good parson, the intriguing woman from the court, the old schoolmaster enraged at a new departure in education, the quack doctor sentenced to dig the graves of those he kills, and many more, stand out from these pages in as sharp relief as words can well paint them. The action is all intense. The bailiff's wife runs home from church as fast as her legs can carry her; her husband is repeatedly so terrified he cannot speak; and his accomplice rolls on the floor in his remorse, and beats himself with his fists. The death of Rudy's mother is full of pathos. The pursuit of Hummel by the devil is extremely humorous; the scene under the gallows, where he confesses himself willing to die, and where his fingers are indelibly stained, is very impressive.

Moreover, as a picture of a somewhat primitive village community, the story is replete with interest and instruction. The
large public square where the people assemble; the extensive
common, the division of which among individual proprietors is
one thread of interest throughout the book; the public hangman's tree; the bailiff beer-house keeper, with everybody in his
debt, listening at the windows, extracting the domestic secrets
of all his customers; the petty thieveries and deceits and
superstitions; the intrigues, scandals, lies, amidst which nothing
thrived but the beer-house; and lastly the great, beneficent magistrate in the old manor-house in the distant background, watching like a good Providence over all the affairs of the hamlet,
and meting out justice in the market, and whom no one could
deceive or thwart, — these scenes are all as strange to us as they
were real to Pestalozzi. The art, in a word, reminds one of
that of the large, colored charts, for combined language and
object teaching, on the walls of so many German schoolrooms, —
masses of strong colors, a crowd of things and persons, without
attempted art or unity, but far truer to and richer in life, for
a child's eye, than anything in the art galleries. Unlike these
charts, however, it has a purpose which lifts it far above these
details to a moral plain, the highest to which literary art can
attain.

There was one good woman in this dismal hamlet, — Gertrude, the mason's wife, who trudged many miles one day to
see the county magistrate, and beg work for her husband, and
to complain of the bad arts of the wicked bailiff, whose beer
made her husband drunk. Her faltering story was heard, and
her husband obtained the job of building a new church; and
at length, after a long struggle, the bailiff was exposed and fell.
Gertrude had taught her own children home industries and
maxims, hymns, prayers, and cleanliness and courtesy, and finally

allowed the children of a neighbor to come in. An idle man of a noble but decayed family witnessed her home-school, and at length resolved to be a schoolmaster himself. Gertrude could not tell him much of her secret, though occasionally she let fall a "key-word." She felt that the school should stand in the closest relation with home life, and not in opposition to it; that it should be a larger circle drawn about the fireside hearth; that verbal instruction should vanish in the spirit of real activity. The schoolmaster's establishment flourished. The preacher was interested, and realized that his sermons were too refined and doctrinal, and not practical, and changed his style. The whole spirit of home life and of industry gradually revived. A few of the best citizens met weekly to discuss the larger educational question of commercial prosperity. The royal cabinet became interested, studied Bonnal, — which had become the thriftiest hamlet in Switzerland, — and at length concluded, that, if the ministry of a realm should seriously and deeply desire reform, they could set about it in no better or more radical way than by imitating Bonnal. Here was, in fact, the principle of universal government.

Thus Bonnal is the world; the bailiff is intemperance, intrigue, and all influences which degrade society; and Gertrude is the Good Teacher by whom alone the world is to be saved, if it is to be saved at all. We shall not read this story as we ought if we forget that there are hundreds of communities in our land to-day in the same need as was Bonnal of a regeneration so radical that only these same slow methods of practical, ethical education can ever accomplish it. Such a regeneration is not to be effected by endowments, legislation, or by new methods, important as these are, but, as Pestalozzi thought, by the love and devotion of noble women overflowing from the domestic circle into the community, by the good Gertrudes of all stations in life, the born educators of the race, whose work and whose "key-words" we men-pedagogues must ponder well if our teaching is to be ethically inspired.

This book represents the culmination of Pestalozzi's influence. Royal personages came to see him, and gave him presents. Herbart, Fichte, and many others, lit their torches at the fire he kindled here. This is a book which all good teachers should read with care, and, having read it, will thank the translator for the great and discriminating labor she has spent upon the very voluminous and intractable original in converting it into the present pleasing form.

G. STANLEY HALL.

JOHNS HOPKINS UNIVERSITY,
March 4, 1885.

CONTENTS.

———•◇•———

LEONARD AND GERTRUDE.

CHAPTER I

A WEAK MAN, A BRAVE WOMAN, AND A FATHERLY RULER.

IN the village of Bonnal there lived a mason named
Leonard. His trade would have enabled him to sup-
port his family of a wife and seven children, if he could
have resisted the temptation to frequent the tavern, where
there were always enough idle loafers to entice him in, and
induce the good-natured, easy-going man to squander his
earnings in drink and gambling. Leonard always repented
his weakness when he saw his children want for bread, yet
was not strong enough to reform. He was blest with a
good, pious wife, who was overwhelmed with sorrow at the
ruin which seemed to stare them in the face.

Gertrude had always contrived to conceal her sadness
from the children, but one day, when her husband remained
away from home longer than usual, she was so overcome
with anxiety and grief that the little ones saw her weep.
"You are crying, mother!" they exclaimed in chorus, and
crowding about her, added their tears to hers. Even the
baby in her arms seemed to feel a premonition of sorrow,
and looked up in her face for the first time without a smile.
This was too much for the afflicted mother, who now wept
aloud, accompanied by the sobs of the children. Their
grief was at its height when the door opened, and Leonard

entered. Gertrude's face was hidden, and the children were clinging about her, too much engrossed with their mother's distress to notice the approach of their father.

"Merciful heavens, what is it?" he cried, turning pale as death. They looked up at the sound of his voice, and the violence of their lamentation ceased. "Gertrude, what dreadful sorrow is this?" he asked again.

"Dear husband, heavy cares oppress my heart, and when you are away, my misery is still greater."

"Gertrude," said Leonard; "I know why you weep,— wretch that I am!"

She led the children away, and Leonard laid his head in her lap without speaking. The quiet was broken only by his sobs, for Gertrude was praying silently. Finally she spoke: "Leonard, trust in God's mercy, and take courage to do right!"

"O Gertrude!" was all he could say amid his tears.

"Take courage, dear," she repeated, "and trust in your Father in heaven. I would not willingly grieve you, and you well know that I do not ask for more than bread and water at your side; and that I often work uncomplainingly till long past midnight for you and the children. But, husband, I should not feel I was true to you or our dear ones if I concealed my cares from you. Our children are loving and dutiful now; but they will not remain so if we do not fulfil our obligation as parents. Think how you would feel if all our little ones should lose their gratitude and respect for us through our fault! And could you bear to see your Nicholas, your Jonas, your Lizzie and Annie, homeless and forced to seek their bread among strangers? It would kill me!" and her tears flowed as she spoke.

Leonard wept also. "O Gertrude, what shall I do? It breaks my heart to make you miserable, but I cannot help it. I owe the Bailiff Hummel thirty florins, and if I stay away from his tavern, he threatens me with the law; yet if I go, he gets possession of all my wages."

"Can you not go to Arner, the people's father? All the widows and orphans praise him, and I think he would give you advice and protection."

"Gertrude, I dare not! How could I, a poor miserable drunkard, complain of the Bailiff, who has a thousand ways of blackening me in the eyes of his superior? And think how he would revenge himself if I should try it and fail!"

"But he will ruin you in any case. Leonard, think of your children, and go. If you do not, I shall!"

"I dare not! But, Gertrude, if you have the courage, go to Arner in Heaven's name, and tell him all."

"I will!" she answered. She prayed throughout the sleepless night, and the next morning took her blooming baby and walked two long hours to the Castle.

The nobleman was sitting under a linden-tree at the gate, and saw her as she approached, with tears in her eyes and the infant on her arm. "Who are you, my daughter, and what do you wish?" he asked, in so kind a tone that she took heart to answer: "I am Gertrude, wife of the mason Leonard in Bonnal."

"You are a good woman," said Arner. "I have noticed that your children behave better than all the others in the village, and they seem better fed, although I hear you are very poor. What can I do for you, my daughter?"

"O gracious Sir, for a long time my husband has owed thirty florins to the Bailiff Hummel, a hard man, who leads him into all sorts of temptation. Leonard is in his power: so he dares not keep away from the tavern, where day after day he spends the wages which ought to buy bread for his family. We have seven little children, Sir, and unless something is done we shall all be beggars. I ventured to come to you for help, because I know that you have compassion for

the widowed and fatherless. I have brought the money I
have laid aside for my children, to deposit with you, if you
will be so good as to make some arrangement so that the
Bailiff shall not torment my husband any more until he is
paid."

Arner took up a cup which stood near, and said to Gertrude : " Drink this tea, and give your pretty baby some of
this milk." She blushed, and was moved even to tears by
his fatherly kindness.

The nobleman now requested her to relate her causes of
complaint against the Bailiff, and listened attentively to her
story of the cares and troubles of many years. Suddenly
he asked her how it had been possible to lay aside money for
her children in the midst of her distress.

"It was very hard, gracious Sir; yet I could not help
feeling as if the money were not mine, but had been given
me by a dying man on his death-bed, in trust for his children. So when in the hardest times I had to borrow from it
to buy bread for the family, I gave myself no rest till by
working late and early I had paid it back again."

Gertrude laid seven neat packages on the table, each of
which had a ticket attached, saying whose it was ; and if she
had taken anything from it, the fact was noted, and likewise
when she had replaced it. She saw him read these tickets
through attentively, and said blushing : "I ought to have
taken those papers away, gracious Sir."

Arner only smiled, and admired the modesty which shrank
from even merited praise. He added something to each
parcel, saying : " Carry back your children's money, Gertrude ; I will lay aside thirty florins until the Bailiff is paid.
Now go home ; I shall be in the village to-morrow, at all
events, and will settle the matter with Hummel."

" God reward you, gracious Sir ! " she faltered ; and
started joyfully with her baby on the long homeward way.

Leonard saw her as she approached the house. "Already back again?" he cried. "You have been successful with Arner."

"How do you know?"

"I can see it in your face, my dear wife,—you cannot deceive me."

From this time forward, when the mason's children said their prayers at morning and evening, they prayed not only for their father and mother, but also for Arner, the people's father.

CHAPTER II.

A TYRANT APPEARS, AND FINDS HIS MASTER.

THAT evening, when the Bailiff went to Arner for orders, the latter remarked: "I am coming to Bonnal myself to-morrow; I want to arrange about the building of the church."

"Is your Grace's master-mason at liberty now, gracious Sir?"

"No; but there is a mason in your village, named Leonard, whom I should be glad to employ. Why have you never recommended him to me before?"

With a low bow the Bailiff replied: "I should not have dared to recommend the poor mason for any of your Worship's buildings."

"Is he a reliable man?"

"Yes, your Grace may depend upon him; he is faithfulness itself."

"They say he has an excellent wife; are you sure she is no busybody?" inquired Arner with emphasis.

"No; she is really a quiet, industrious woman."

"Very well; be at the churchyard at nine to-morrow morning. I will meet you there."

Soon after this conversation, the Bailiff was knocking violently at the door of the mason's little hut, where Leonard and Gertrude were still sitting at the supper-table. The mason recognized the voice of the envious Bailiff, and hastily pushing the food into a corner, he turned deadly pale as he went to open the door.

Like a hungry hound, the Bailiff scented the hidden viands, but spoke with feigned friendliness: "You are having an easy time, my good people; it's not so hard to do without the tavern, is it, Leonard?"

The mason cast down his eyes in silence, but Gertrude was bolder. "What are your commands, Sir Bailiff?" she said. "I wonder you should come nearer than the window of so poor a house as this."

Concealing his anger, Hummel answered with a smile: "It is true I should not have expected to find such good fare here, or I might have called oftener."

This irritated Gertrude. "Bailiff!" she exclaimed, "you smell our supper, and grudge it to us. You ought to be ashamed to spoil a poor man's meal, when perhaps he doesn't get so good a one three times a year."

"That was not my intention," returned the magistrate, still with a smile. But the next moment he added seriously: "You are too inclined to be insolent, Gertrude, which does not become poor people. It might be worth your while to reflect that you may perhaps have some dealings with me yet, — but enough of that! I am always well disposed toward your husband, and can give you proofs of it."

"My husband is enticed into drinking and gaming every day in your tavern, and afterwards I with my children have to suffer every misery at home; *that* is the service we owe you!"

"You wrong me, Gertrude. It is true your husband is rather a sorry fellow, and I have told him so myself; but in my tavern I must give food and drink to every one who asks for it. Everybody does the same."

"Yes; but not everybody threatens a poor man with the law, if he does not double his debts every year."

Furiously the Bailiff turned to Leonard. "Are these the sort of tales you tell of me, you rascal? It's lucky I have all your bills and memoranda in my hands! Perhaps you will venture to dispute my claims?"

"That would not enter my head," said Leonard. "Ger-trude is only anxious for me to make no new debts."

Controlling himself, Hummel observed in a milder tone: "There's no great harm in that; but you are the man of the house, and she certainly will not want to tie you to her apron-strings."

"By no means, Bailiff," said Gertrude. "On the con-trary, I would like to free him from the bonds which already hold him; that is, your book, Sir Bailiff, and your fine mem-oranda."

"He has only to pay me, and then he will be free as air."

"That he will be able to do,. if he makes no fresh debts."

"You are proud, Gertrude, — but we will see! I imagine you would rather have your husband feast at home with you than drink a glass of wine with me."

"That is contemptible, Bailiff! but your words have no power to hurt me."

Hummel could bear it no longer, and took an abrupt leave, wondering what could have occurred to make Gertrude so bold. It was almost midnight before he reached home, but he sent immediately for two of Leonard's neighbors, who rose from their beds and came at once, in obedience to his summons. The Bailiff questioned them narrowly concerning the pursuits of the mason's family during the last few days, and when nothing came to light which could explain the mystery, he flew into a violent passion. "You dogs! There is no getting anything out of you! And yet when you carry off whole cartloads of wood from Arner's premises, and turn your cattle into his pastures to graze, you expect me to say nothing about it! Buller, more than a third of your reckoning was false, but I was silent. And Krüel, half of your meadow belongs by good rights to your brother's chil-

dren, — what if I should have· you hung, as you richly de-
serve?"

This threat seemed to stimulate Krüel's memory, for he at
once began: "Stop a minute, Bailiff, — I think I can help
you. It just crosses my mind that Gertrude was away all
this morning; and to-night her Lizzie was praising Arner at
the well; she must have been at the Castle. Then last night
there was a loud sound of crying from their house, and to-
day they are all as merry as larks."

The Bailiff dismissed his informants, bidding them keep
silence in regard to their discoveries, and do their best to
bring him fresh information as soon as possible. In the
morning he went again to the mason's house, and after a
friendly greeting, said: "Leonard, we parted in anger last
night, but that must not be. I have good news for you. I
have just been with our gracious master, who was talking
about building the church. He asked about you, and I told
him I thought you were equal to the undertaking; so I think
he will give it to you."

"But he arranged with his master-mason about the building, — you said so yourself long ago."

"I thought it was so, but I was mistaken; the mason only
made an estimate of expenses, and didn't forget himself,
you may believe. If you can get the job on the basis of
this calculation, you will hook in your money by the armful.
Now you can judge whether I am your friend or not!"

The mason was so happy that he thanked the Bailiff grate-
fully; but Gertrude saw plainly that their treacherous guest
already had an eye to the wages her husband would earn in
his new employment. As he departed, the Bailiff remarked:
"Arner will be here in an hour"; and Lizzie, who stood by
her father's side, spoke up: "Yes, we have known that since
yesterday." Hummel started at the words, but paid no attention to them.

In the mean time, Arner had reached the churchyard, where a crowd of the villagers had assembled to look on their good master. "Have you nothing to do, or is it a holiday, that you all have time to loaf about here?" asked the Bailiff of those who stood nearest; but Arner said aloud: " Bailiff, I am very willing for all my children to remain and hear my wishes with regard to the building; why do you drive them away?" Hummel bent himself to the ground, and called out to the neighbors: "Come back, his Grace has no objection."

Arner asked the Bailiff if he had seen the estimate for the building, and whether he thought Leonard could make it good and durable at the given price. "Yes, gracious Sir," replied Hummel, adding in a lower tone: "I think perhaps he might even do it a little cheaper, as he lives in the village."

But Arner said aloud: "I will give him just the same I should have given the master-mason. Send for him, and see that everything is delivered to him from the storehouses which the master-mason would have had."

The messenger soon returned, and the Bailiff turned deadly pale on remarking that he was accompanied by Gertrude, who had decided to come herself in her husband's absence. "What is the matter, Sir Bailiff?" inquired Arner.

"Nothing, gracious Sir; I didn't sleep well last night, that is all."

"You look as if you had not," replied Arner, looking fixedly into his inflamed eyes. Then turning to Gertrude with a pleasant greeting, he asked: "Is not your husband here? But no matter, you can simply tell him to come to me. I am going to intrust the building of the church to him."

Gertrude stood silent, too much abashed to utter a word in the presence of so many people. "Why do you not speak, Gertrude?" said Arner. "You must be delighted to learn that your husband is to have the building on the same terms agreed upon for the master-mason."

Gertrude rallied sufficiently to stammer: "Gracious Sir, the church is so near the tavern!"

Everybody began to laugh, and the Bailiff cried angrily to Gertrude: "What have you against my tavern?"

Arner interrupted him with: "Pray, is this your affair, Bailiff?" and turning to the mason's wife, demanded an explanation of her words.

"Gracious Sir, my husband is easily enticed into drinking, and if he has to work so near the tavern every day, I am afraid he will not be able to resist the temptation. One gets thirsty working, Sir, and if all the time there are people before his eyes drinking and betting, and teasing him to join them, how can he help listening? And if he is once in debt again, it is all over with him. O Sir, if you only knew how a single evening in such a house can bring a man into slavery from which it is hardly possible to escape!"

"I do know it, Gertrude, and I mean to show the whole world that I am not going to let the poor people be oppressed and abused." Then turning to the Bailiff with a penetrating look, he demanded: "Is it true that the poor people are enticed into your house, and then cheated and oppressed?"

Pale as death Hummel stammered: "No, indeed, gracious Sir! That's the reward a man gets for serving beggars!"

"But the question is, whether this woman speaks falsely."

"Indeed she does, gracious Sir! I will prove it in a thousand ways."

"One is quite sufficient, Bailiff. But take care! Yesterday you said Gertrude was an industrious woman, and no busybody."

The Bailiff was so confused at this that he could bring forth no intelligible answer, and Arner turned for confirmation to two old men who stood near. "Is it true, my good neighbors, that people are oppressed and ruined in your tavern?"

The men looked at each other, but did not speak. "Do not be afraid, — tell me the simple truth."

"It is but too true, gracious Sir; but how can *we* complain against the Bailiff?" replied the older of the two, so low that only Arner could distinguish the words.

"It is enough," said the nobleman, turning again to Hummel. "It was not my intention to investigate this complaint to-day, but I am determined to protect my people from every sort of oppression, and I have long thought that no bailiff ought to keep a tavern. But we will postpone that matter until Monday. — Gertrude, tell your husband to come to me, and be quite easy as regards the tavern."

CHAPTER III.

HOW PEASANTS TALK, AND ROGUES PLAN.

THE Bailiff did not go home until evening, and when he approached his house, usually brilliantly lighted, and noisy with the sounds of revelry, he was terrified to observe that all was dark and still. He rushed in, and found no one but his wife, who was sobbing in a corner. "O husband, is that you?" she cried. "What a misfortune has befallen us! All our enemies are exulting, and not a man in the village dares to drink a glass of wine at our house."

Hummel was almost beside himself with rage, and spent a large part of the night in plotting vengeance against the author of his misfortunes. The next morning, however, he resolved to put a good face on the matter, and began whistling merrily under his open window. His neighbor Fritz called out to him: "Have you customers so early, that you are in such good spirits?"

"Oh, they'll be coming before long. Will you drink my health, Fritz?"— holding a glass of brandy out of the window.

"It is too early: I'll wait till there is more company."

"You always were full of your fun. But you needn't think that business of yesterday is going to turn out so badly. No bird flies so high that it doesn't come down again!"

"I don't know about that," remarked Fritz. "The bird I have in mind has had a long enough flight. But we may not be speaking of the same bird. Hallo! They are call-

ing me to breakfast,"—and he closed the window as he
spoke, leaving the Bailiff to no very agreeable reflections.

Soon after, Hummel started for the barber's, with a defi-
nite end in view. On his way he met Nickel Spitz, who thus
accosted him: "Where are you going in your Sunday
clothes, Sir Bailiff?"

"To the barber's."

"It's queer you are at leisure on Saturday morning."

"To be sure, it is not so all the year round; but come
with me,—there will perhaps be some drinking, or fun of
some sort."

"I imagine you would have a reckoning with the barber,
if he had any wine drunk in his house!" exclaimed Nickel.

"I am not so selfish as all that. Indeed, they talk of
taking away my license altogether; but, Nickel, it will be
some time yet before that comes to pass."

"You are about right there. But it isn't the best luck in
the world for you that our young master has a different
creed from his grandfather. I suspect they differed about
every article of the twelve."

"Very possibly," observed Hummel. "Yet the old
man's belief was more to my mind."

"So I should suppose. The first article of his creed
was: 'I believe in you, my Bailiff.'"

"Very good!—and what was the second?"

"How should I know? Possibly something like this: 'I
don't believe a word from any man living *except* you, my
Bailiff.'"

"Really, Nickel, you ought to have been a parson! You
might have set up a new Catechism."

"They would hardly have let me do that. I should have
made it so plain that the children could all have understood
it without any parson, so that there would have been no need
of one at all."

" It is better to stick to the old, Nickel, in the Catechism as in everything else ; we don't better ourselves by changing. But as far as I am concerned, I am not so much afraid of this new master."

" Yet your good luck was buried last summer with his grandfather."

" Well, Nickel, at all events I have had my share of good luck."

" That you have, Sir, — but you couldn't well have helped it. The clerk, the beadle, and the vicar all owed you money."

" Fool ! You don't know as much as you think."

" I know much more than that ! I know what tricks you played on Rudy's father, and how I caught you lying on your face in the straw by the dog-kennel, in front of Rudy's window, while his attorney was with him. You staid there listening to what they said till two o'clock in the morning, and then it was easy enough for you, with the clerk, to distort your own evidence."

" There is not a word of truth in what you say ! "

" There isn't? I tell you if the clerk had not changed your evidence before the court, Rudy would still be in possession of his meadow, and Wüst and Kaibacher would not have had to perjure themselves."

" The best part of it is that I won the lawsuit," remarked the Bailiff. " I shouldn't have liked to have you know I had lost it."

" Oh, yes, I know well enough you won it, and also in what way ! " said Nickel, taking his departure abruptly.

As the Bailiff entered the barber's house, where a number of the neighbors were already assembled, contrary to his wont he greeted them all politely before seating himself ; but the peasants were far less deferential than usual, and plainly showed their distrust of their magistrate. Seeing this, he sent a boy to bring wine from his own house, and placed his well-filled tobacco-pouch on the table. A cloud of smoke soon arose, and amid the clinking of glasses which followed, all prejudices against Hummel were forgotten. The latter had previously arranged with his wife that the wine should be adulterated with brimstone, and also that a jug of colored water should be prepared for his own use. When the heads of the peasants were heated, the Bailiff adroitly turned the conversation to the rights of the people, insinuating that if Arner should get the tavern license into his own hands, the price of wine would soon rise.

Just as the excitement had reached its height, one of the half-intoxicated fellows upset the jug at Hummel's elbow, and the barber's dog, coming up, lapped the colored water from the floor. This aroused the wonder of the peasants, and led to a discovery of the imposture, whereupon so great a tumult arose that the barber requested the rioters to withdraw. The enraged Bailiff invited the company to his own house, but was followed only by two or three good-for-nothing loafers. One of these he at once despatched in pursuit of the mason's apprentice Joseph, who soon made his appearance.

" Good-day, Joseph ! " said the Bailiff ; " does your master know you are here ? "

" He is at the Castle, and will not be back till noon ; so If I am at work again by one o'clock, he will be none the wiser."

" Very well," — and leading him into the adjoining apartment, the Bailiff bolted the door behind them. On the table were pork, sausages, bread, and wine. " Come, Joseph," said his host ; " drink a glass, and try these sausages. Do help yourself ! You have a hard enough time at your master's."

" Yes," was the reply ; " but now he has work, things will go better."

"You are a fool, Joseph! How long do you suppose that will last? He is not a competent man for the job, since he has never had the charge of a large building before. He will depend on you entirely, and for that reason I want to ask a favor of you."

"I am at your service, Sir Bailiff. I drink to you!"

The Bailiff helped him again to sausages, and continued: "I should be glad if the foundation of the church could be of stone from the Schwendi quarry."

"Impossible, Sir Bailiff! You don't know what you are talking about. This stone is good for nothing as a foundation."

"Oh, I hardly think it is so bad; I have seen it used for many purposes. Joseph, I should regard it as a personal favor if this quarry could be used."

"But the walls will rot away in six years' time if they are made of this stone."

"That is all nonsense! And after all, what concern is it of yours whether the walls are sound ten years from now? Just do as I say, and you shall have reason to be glad of it."

"But suppose Arner should notice that the stone is good for nothing? He knows more about some things than you would think."

"Pooh! He knows nothing of that. Just give me your hand on it, and if your master takes the stone from that quarry, you shall have five thalers for yourself."

The bargain was concluded, when the Bailiff added: "One thing more, Joseph. I have a little bag of stuff from the apothecary, which is said to make mortar stick to a wall like iron, if it is mixed with the lime. But I should like to try it on some other building before I use it on any of my own."

"All right! I'll try it for you on the corner of a neighbor's house."

"No, Joseph; that would be no test at all. I would like to have it tried on the church-tower. Isn't that possible?"

"Is it necessary to put much into the lime?" asked the apprentice.

"A couple of pounds to a barrel, I suppose."

"That is easy enough."

"Then you will do it?"

"To be sure."

"And hold your tongue if it fails?"

"Of course I shall hold my tongue; and it can't fail."

"Well, come and get the stuff from me when you need it, and a glass of wine into the bargain."

"All right, Sir Bailiff. To your health, and my best thanks!" cried Joseph, quaffing a parting glass.

CHAPTER IV.

HOME JOYS.

MEANWHILE, Gertrude had been hurrying to finish her
Saturday's work before Leonard came back from the Castle.
While combing and braiding the children's hair, mending
their clothes, and putting the room to rights, she had taught
the little ones a song, with which to greet their father on his
return. As the mason entered, wife and children sang in
chorus : —

> "Gentle peace, who art from heaven,
>   Soothing every pain and care,
>   Healing with the sweetest balsam
>   Those who most are in despair,
>   I am weary of this striving,
>   I am longing for a rest, —
>   Higher thou than pain or pleasure,
>   Come and dwell within my breast!"

"God bless you!" cried Leonard, with tears in his eyes.

"My dear husband," said Gertrude, "earth becomes
heaven when we seek for peace, do right, and wish for
little."

"If I ever enjoy this heaven on earth, I owe it to you!
I shall thank you all my life for saving me, and so will our
little ones. — Children, do right, and follow in your mother's
footsteps ; then you will prosper."

"You seem in good spirits to-day," remarked Gertrude
presently.

"I have had a successful interview with Arner. To think
how childishly I behaved about going to him!"

"It is always easy enough to be wise after the event. But now tell me the whole story," she besought, taking up her knitting.

"But, my dear wife, it is Saturday, and you wouldn't have time to hear it all."

"Just look about you," said Gertrude, with a smile.

"She has hurried, father," spoke up Lizzie. "Annie and I helped her clear up."

"Now do begin!" begged Gertrude.

"Well, Arner even asked me my father's name, and what street I live in, and the number of my house."

"I know better, Leonard! That certainly was not the way he began."

"Why not, you little wise head?"

"You first greeted him, and he thanked you. Tell me about that!"

"You witch! you are quite right; I didn't begin at the beginning. Well, he asked me first of all whether I was still afraid of him. I made my best bow, and said: 'Forgive me, gracious Sir!' Then he laughed, and had a jug of wine set before me."

"That is quite a different beginning! I'll warrant it did not take you long to dispose of the wine."

"You are wrong, wife. I was bashful as a young bride, and would not touch it. But he bade me pour it out, and I drank his health, although he looked at me so steadily that the glass shook in my hand."

"Your conscience pricked you at the tips of your fingers, Leonard! But you recovered, I suppose?"

"Yes, very soon. He was very kind, and said: 'It is quite natural for a hard-working man to like a glass of wine, and there is no objection to his having it; but it is a misfortune when a man makes a fool of himself over his wine, and forgets his family and the future.' Wife, those words seemed to stab me to the heart. He went on to say how unfortunate it was that poor people, when they are in trouble, usually get into the hands of the very persons they ought to avoid like the plague, and then have neither the sense nor the courage to tell their situation to those who would be glad to help them. ' Mason,' he said, ' just think what would have been the upshot of your difficulties, if your wife had had no more courage and common sense than you!'"

" And he said all this," observed Gertrude, " before asking the number of the house? You didn't mean to tell me of it, you scamp!"

" I think it might have been wiser if I had not, for you will be growing much too vain on account of your courage."

" Do you think so, my good sir? Well, I do believe I shall pride myself all my life on this deed of mine. But what did Arner say next?"

"Oh, he examined me in regard to the building. I had to reckon up every single item of the expense, even to the bringing of lime and sand and stone."

" I hope you made no mistakes."

" No, not this time, my love. And guess how much he has given me in advance"—jingling the coins in his pocket. " It is a long time since we have heard the sound of so much silver." Gertrude sighed. " Don't sigh, my love! We will be prudent and saving, and shall surely never be in such distress again."

" Yes, God in heaven has helped us," she murmured.

" And many more in the village beside. Only think, he has chosen ten fathers of families as laborers on the building, and will give them each twenty-five kreutzers a day. He asked how many children they each had, and what was their trade, and then picked out those who were worst off, and had the most young children. He asked me if I knew anybody who was in trouble, as I had been, and I mentioned Hübel-Rudy ; so he is sure of work for a year."

" That was very right of you, not to let Rudy suffer for taking your potatoes."

" I couldn't bear a grudge against a poor man, wife, — and they are in a wretched condition. I found Rudy a few days ago near the potato-bin, and I pretended not to see him. He was the picture of want, and we have always had something to eat."

" That is all very well, my dear husband. But stealing doesn't help people out of their misery, and those who do it only become doubly wretched."

" True ; but when a man is suffering the pangs of hunger, and sees food before him ; when he knows how much of it must rot in the bins, and that even the cattle have enough to eat, — O Gertrude ! what strength of mind it takes to let it lie and not touch it ! "

" It is hard indeed ; yet the poor man must be able to do it, or he cannot help being miserable. But, Leonard, have you looked to see whether the men are at work? I didn't tell you that Joseph stole away to the tavern again to-day."

" How vexatious ! The Bailiff must have sent for him. I stopped to speak to the men on my way home, and if he was fresh from the tavern, what he said makes me uneasy."

" What was it ? "

" He said the stone from the Schwendi quarry would be excellent for the church-wall ; and when I told him that the great flint stones which lie about in great quantity were much better, he said I must always be a fool, and never know my own advantage. But this Schwendi stone is soft and sandy, and not at all fit for this work. If he has been with the Bailiff, there is something behind it all. Suppose it should be a trap ! "

" Beware of Joseph, he is not reliable," warned Gertrude

" They won't catch me so easily! Arner doesn't want any sandstone in the foundation: he said it would decay and be corroded by saltpetre, because there are dung-heaps and stable drainage down by the wall. It is wonderful how perfectly he understands everything! While we were talking, Lord Oberhofen was announced, and I thought I ought to say I would not detain him, but would come another day. Arner laughed, and said: ' No, mason, I like to finish what I am about, and wait till I have done with one person before attending to another. This is part of your old shiftless ways, to leave your work on the slightest provocation.' I scratched my ear rather foolishly, wife, and wished I had held my tongue."

" He wasn't so far out of the way," said Gertrude with a laugh.

CHAPTER V.

THE DEATH-BED OF A GOOD WOMAN.

As soon as Leonard had left the Castle, Arner despatched a messenger to the Bailiff with the list of laborers, and orders to notify them of their employment. All previous letters from Arnheim had been directed: "To the honorable and discreet, my dear and faithful Bailiff Hummel in Bonnal;" but the present communication bore the simple address: "To the Bailiff Hummel in Bonnal." "What does that confounded secretary mean by not giving me my proper title?" growled the magistrate.

"Take care, Bailiff!" cried Flink, the messenger. "It was our lord and master himself who directed the letter."

"Impossible! I know the writing of that powdered beggar of a secretary."

"That is going rather too far, Mr. Bailiff; for I stood by when Arner wrote the address, and saw him do it with my own eyes."

"Then I have made an infernal blunder, Flink! Forget all about it, and come in and drink a glass of wine with me."

After the mollified messenger had taken his departure, the Bailiff ran his eye over the list, and muttered: "They are all loafers and beggars, from beginning to end, — not a single one of them my men, except Michael. And I am to notify them all to-day! All right! I will advise them at the same time to go to the Castle on Monday, and thank their benefactor. Arner doesn't know one of the fellows, and when they come before him, all in tatters, one without shoes, and another minus a hat, I am mistaken if I haven't the best of the joke on my side."

He planned the order of his visits, and resolved to go first to Hübel-Rudy, so as to have it over; for he had dreaded to approach the house ever since the lawsuit by which he had defrauded Rudy's father of the meadow. Rudy was sitting with his children. It was but three months since his wife's death, and now his mother lay dying on a bed of straw. "Do get me some leaves for my coverlet this afternoon, — I am cold!" she said to her son.

"Yes, mother; as soon as the fire is out, I will go."

"Have you any more wood, Rudy? I fear not, for you cannot leave me and the children to go after any. O Rudy, I have lived to be a burden to you!"

"No, mother, do not say that! You are never a burden to me. If I could only give you what you need! You are hungry and thirsty and sick, and I, wretched man, can do nothing for you."

"Do not grieve, Rudy. God will soon relieve my suffering, and as we draw near our end, we want little more on earth."

"But, mother," he cried weeping, "don't you think you will get well again?"

"No, Rudy, I am certain I shall not. But be comforted, my son! You have been the joy of my youth and the comfort of my old age. I will pray to God for you, and all your sufferings will end in good."

"My dear, dear mother!" was all that he could say.

"Rudy," she began presently, "I have just one thing on my mind before I die. Yesterday I saw our little Rudy hide behind my bed and eat roasted potatoes out of his pocket. He gave some to the other children, and they all eat them on the sly. Rudy, those potatoes cannot be our own, else he would have brought me some, as he used to do. How

pleased I always was when he came running to me with
something in his hand, and cried in his affectionate way:
' You eat some, grandma! ' O Rudy, to think of this darling child becoming a thief! Bring him to me."

As the boy approached her bed, she raised herself with
an effort, and took both his hands in hers. The child
sobbed aloud. " What do you want, grandma? Don't die,
grandma! "

" Yes, my little Rudy, I must soon die," she answered
brokenly. The exertion had been too great, and she sank
back upon the bed exhausted.

" I will die with you, grandma! " cried the little fellow,
weeping.

" No, my Rudy; God grant you may live many years,
and grow up to be a help and comfort to your father when
he is old and weak. Promise me, my dear boy, that you
will follow his example, and grow up a good man."

" Yes, grandma, I promise."

" And Rudy dear, the Father to whom I am now going
sees everything we do, and hears all the promises we make.
Do you know that? "

" Yes, grandma."

" Then why did you eat stolen potatoes yesterday behind
my bed? "

" O grandma, do forgive me! I will never, never do so
any more! "

" From whom did you steal them? "

" From the mason," sobbed the child.

" You must go to him, and ask his forgiveness; and in
future, even if you are hungry, trust the dear God, and do
not steal."

" No, grandma, I will never, never steal again, even if I
am hungry."

" Then may God bless and keep you, my dear boy! " she

cried, pressing him to her heart. " But now you must go to the mason. — Go with him, my son, and tell them I too implore their forgiveness, and only wish I could give back the potatoes. Say to them I will pray for a blessing on what they have left. It grieves me to the heart, they have so much need of all they have, and would not be able to make both ends meet, with their large family, if Gertrude did not work night and day. Rudy, I know you will work for him a couple of days, to make it up."

" With all my heart, my dear mother."

At this moment there was a tap on the window outside, and the sick woman recognized the Bailiff's cough. " Merciful heavens!" she exclaimed, " it is the Bailiff! I am afraid the bread and butter from which you are preparing my broth are not paid for."

" Do not worry, mother! I will work for him, and reap for him at harvest-time," — and Rudy ran out of the room.

The old woman sighed, and murmured : " Since the lawsuit (God forgive him!) the sight of him always stabs me to the heart. And to think that he must imbitter my last hour by standing under my window! It is God's will that I should forgive him wholly, and pray for the welfare of his soul, and I will do it." She heard the Bailiff talking in loud tones outside. " Good heavens, he is angry!" she cried; and as his voice again reached her ears, she fainted away. Little Rudy ran to the door, and called: "Come, father, come! I think grandma is dead!"

" Merciful God!" exclaimed Rudy. " Bailiff, I must go in."

" There is great need of that!" muttered Hummel; " it would be a terrible loss, indeed, if the old witch should be dead at last!"

But Rudy did not hear his words, for he had rushed into the house. The dying woman soon regained consciousness,

and inquired as she opened her eyes: "Was he angry,
Rudy? I am sure he would not wait, and has threatened you
with the law."

"No, mother, it is good news; he gave me notice that I
am to be one of the day-laborers at the building of the
church, and we are each to have twenty-five kreutzers a day."
"Can that be really true? Then I shall die happier.
Great God, thou art merciful!" Here her breath began to
fail, and she took leave of her sorrowing son with courage
and cheerfulness, invoking a blessing upon his head, and
giving him a message of forgiveness for the Bailiff. Then
she summoned the weeping children to her bedside, and
spoke words of solace and counsel, leaving them her two
Bibles and prayer-books as a remembrance.

After the sick woman had ceased speaking, the children and
their father remained for some time on their knees, praying,
until Rudy finally arose and said: "Mother, I will go now
and get the leaves for your coverlet."

"There is no hurry about that," she answered; "the room
is warmer now, and you must go with the child to the
mason's."

Gertrude was alone in the house when they came, and saw
that both the boy and his father had tears in their eyes.
"What is the matter, neighbor Rudy? Why are you both
weeping?" — and she took the child kindly by the hand.

"Alas, Gertrude, I am in trouble," answered Hübel-Rudy.
"In his hunger, our little Rudy has taken potatoes from
your bin several times. Forgive us, Gertrude! His grandmother found it out yesterday, and he has confessed. She
lies on her death-bed, and has just taken leave of us; she
adds her prayer for forgiveness to ours."

"Say no more, Rudy.—And you, my dear little fellow,
come here and promise me never to take anything from anybody again. Come to me, if you are hungry, and if I can,

I will give you something." She bent down and kissed him, adding: " You have a dear, good grandmother; try to grow up as pious and upright as she."

" Please forgive me!" implored the boy; "I will never steal again."

" Thank God, I now have work at the church," said his father, " and I hope he will not be tempted by hunger to do such a thing again."

Gertrude only said: " My husband and I were very glad that Arner chose you for one of the workmen."

" And I am so glad," cried Rudy, "that my mother lived to know this consolation! Tell your husband I will work for him early and late, and would like to have the price of the potatoes deducted from my wages."

" Nonsense, Rudy! My husband will do no such thing. Heaven be praised, we are also better off on account of the building." She filled the child's pocket with dried fruit, and after helping his father gather leaves for the coverlet, accompanied him to his mother's bedside. Her eyes filled with tears as she took the dying woman's hand in hers.

" You are weeping, Gertrude?" said Rudy's mother. " It is we who should weep. Have you forgiven us?"

" Speak no more of that, Catharine! I only wish I could do something for you in your sickness."

" You are very good, Gertrude; but God will soon help me. — My little Rudy, has she forgiven you?"

" Yes, grandma; just see how good she is!" — displaying the contents of his pocket.

" I am drowsy," murmured the sick woman, "and my eyes are growing dim. Gertrude, I wanted to ask something of you, but I hardly dare. This unhappy child has stolen from you; may I ask, Gertrude — when — I am dead — these poor, motherless children — may I hope — that you" — Her eyes were already closed, and in a few moments she breathed her last.

Gertrude tried to comfort poor Rudy, and repeated the last words of his mother, which he had not caught. He grasped her hand. "O Gertrude, how good my mother was! Tell me, you will remember her last wish?"

"I should have a heart of stone if I could forget it. I will do what I can for your children." Then she kissed little Rudy and the others, prepared the corpse for burial, and did not go home until everything was done which was necessary.

CHAPTER VI.

REPENTANCE, HYPOCRISY, ROGUERY, AND FALSE PRIDE.

The Bailiff continued his round of visits, meeting with various receptions from the different peasants to whose doors his errand carried him. In every instance he encountered astonishment, amounting often to incredulity, which in most cases gave place to joy and thankfulness as the poor men realized their good fortune. On his way to one of the houses, the Bailiff came unexpectedly upon Hans Wüst. "Is it you, Wüst?" he cried. "Have you quite forgotten the money I lent you?"

"I have no money now, and when I come to think of it, I am afraid I have paid too dearly for your money already."

"Nonsense, Wüst! On my soul, I tell you that you only swore to what I read aloud to you a hundred times, — and you said each time: 'Oh, yes, I can swear to that!' But you only say this on account of the debt, so that I shall let you wait longer."

"No, Bailiff, you are wrong. If I had the money, I would fling it at your feet, so that I might never have to look you in the face again. I tried to see the matter as you did, although I was conscious all the time that our gracious master understood it differently."

"What business was it of yours what he understood? You swore to nothing that was not true."

"No, Bailiff, it was a base deceit. Poor Rudy! Everywhere I go, I see him before me, and his poor, sickly chil-

dren, who were once so healthy and blooming, before I swore
that false oath which took his meadow from him."

"But you didn't say it was not his, or that it was mine.
What is it to you in the Devil's name to whom the meadow
belongs?"

"It is nothing to me to whom the meadow belongs, but
everything to me that I have sworn falsely, God forgive me!"

"But I tell you, you didn't swear falsely, Wüst! Now
just drive it out of your head, and come in and drink a glass
of wine with me, to cheer you up!"

"No, Bailiff. Nothing on earth can make me cheerful
now."

"Nonsense! See, here is your note, and I will tear it up
before your eyes. I will take the responsibility of the matter
on my own shoulders."

"Take what responsibility you will! But day after to-
morrow I shall sell my Sunday coat, and pay your debt."

"Don't be such a fool, Wüst! But I must be going."

"It is a mercy! For if you staid any longer, I should
go mad before your eyes."

They separated, and the Bailiff went on in no very comfortable frame of mind to the house of Felix Kriecher. The
latter was a man of sanctimonious appearance and deferential manners, who attended all the sermons and church exer-
cises, and courted favor especially with the pietists of the
village, without, however, attaining to more than partial success in that quarter, since he was not willing to sacrifice his
good standing among the remaining villagers for their sake.
His private virtues, which were reserved strictly for the
home circle, consisted in making the lives of his wife and
children miserable. In their greatest poverty he always
demanded something good to eat, and unless he obtained it,
found fault with everything. If there was nothing else to
criticise, and his little four-year-old happened to look at him

askance, he would strike the tiny hands with violence, "to teach it proper respect." "You are a fool!" said his wife on one of these occasions. He kicked her in return for this truthful statement, so that she stumbled and fell, receiving two severe wounds in her head. This alarmed the hypocrite for his own reputation, and he begged his wife, on his knees, to tell no one the circumstances. The poor woman complied, and told the neighbors she had had a fall; but Kriecher had forgotten the wound almost before it was healed.

A quarter of an hour before the Bailiff's visit, the cat had upset the oil lamp, which stood on the stove, and a few drops had been spilled. "Idiot! Why didn't you train her better than that?" he cried in fury to his wife. "Now you can sit in the dark, and light the fire with cow-dung, you horned beast!" The woman was silent, but tears flowed down her cheeks, and the children were crying in the corners, when there came a knock at the door. "Silence, for Heaven's sake!" exclaimed Kriecher menacingly. He wiped the children's tears with his handkerchief, threatening to cut any one of them to pieces that dared to whimper, and then opened the door to the Bailiff with a low bow. In a few words Hummel explained his errand. Kriecher listened, and as all seemed still within the room, he made answer: "Come in, Sir Bailiff! I want to tell my dear wife at once what a piece of good fortune has befallen me."

They entered, and the hypocrite announced the joyful tidings. "Thank God!" said the poor woman, with an involuntary sigh.

"Is anything the matter with your wife?" inquired the Bailiff.

"I grieve to say she has not been quite well for some time past," replied Kriecher, with an angry glance in the direction of his victim. "But, Sir Bailiff, might I ask you to be so good as to thank our gracious master in my name for this favor?"

" You can do so yourself."

" You are right, Sir Bailiff.   It was a great liberty on my part to ask you to do it.   I will go to the Castle within a day or two, — I feel it to be my duty."

" Monday morning all the others are going, and you might go with them."

" Certainly I will.   My best thanks to you, Sir Bailiff."

" You have no occasion to thank me," replied the magistrate, taking his departure.   Soon after, he sought out the rogue Michael, a man after his own heart, who came to meet him with the salutation : " What the Devil are you up to now?"

" Something jolly," answered Hummel.

" You are the sort of fellow they would be likely to send out to invite people to weddings, dances, and jollifications generally ! "

" At all events my errand is no melancholy one."

" Well, what is it?"

" You have got into new company."

" Who are they? "

" Hübel-Rudy, Leuk, Leemann, Kriecher, Marx, and some others."

" Nonsense !   What am I to do in company with them? "

" Build up and adorn the house of the Lord in Bonnal."

" In sober earnest? "

" As I'm a living sinner."

" But who has chosen the halt and the lame for such a purpose? "

" Our high-born, sagacious, and august master, Arner," replied the Bailiff.

" Is he a fool? "

" How should I know? "

" It looks like it."

" Perhaps it wouldn't be the worst thing in the world if

he were! But I must be going. Come to my house this evening, Michael; I want to have a talk with you."

The Bailiff next went to Marx, formerly a well-to-do merchant, whose property had long since come under the hammer, and who now lived wholly upon the charity of the parson and a few rich relations. In the depth of his poverty, however, he retained his pride, and concealed his destitute condition most carefully from all except those who aided him. He started when he saw the Bailiff, and hustled the rags which lay about, under the bed-quilt, ordering the almost naked children to hide themselves in the adjoining room.

"But, father!" they cried; "it snows and rains in! Just hear what a storm it is, and there is no window in the room now."

"Go along, you wretched children, or you will drive me distracted! Do you think there is no need of your learning to mortify the flesh?" — and pushing them in, he fastened the door, and then invited the Bailiff into the room.

On hearing the announcement, Marx inquired: "Am I to be the overseer among these men?"

"What are you thinking of, Marx? You are workman, like all the rest, and are free to take or leave the job as you see fit."

"I have not been accustomed to such work; but since it is under Arner and the pastor, I can't very well decline."

"They will be greatly rejoiced, and I am almost inclined to think Arner will send me back to thank you."

"I don't mean exactly that; but generally speaking, I wouldn't like to serve under everybody as day-laborer."

"Then you don't lack for bread," observed the Bailiff.

"I never have yet, thank God!"

"So I supposed. But where are your children?"

"With my sainted wife's sister; they dine at her house."

"I thought I heard children crying in the next room."

" There isn't one of them at home."

But the Bailiff heard the same sound again, and, opening the door without ceremony, beheld the almost naked children, with chattering teeth, shivering in the wind, which drove the rain and snow into the half ruined apartment. " Is this where your children dine, Marx?" he asked.

" For Heaven's sake, tell nobody of it, Bailiff! I should be the most miserable man under the sun, if it should become known!"

" Are you beside yourself, Marx? Why don't you tell them to come out? Don't you see they are blue with the cold? I wouldn't treat my dog so!"

" Well, then, children, come out! But, Bailiff, for Heaven's sake, tell nobody!"

" And you play the saint before the pastor, you pious old infidel! It was you who told him about the row last week, —you, and no other! You were going home past my house at twelve o'clock, from some pious feast or other."

" No, as sure as I live, Bailiff, that is not true! May I never stir from this spot again if it is!"

" Marx, will you maintain what you have just said before the parson's face in my presence?" Marx stammered and grew confused. " Such a brute and a liar as you I never met before!" said the Bailiff; and before an hour had passed, he related the whole story to the pastor's cook, who promised to report it to her master. The Bailiff rejoiced to think that the clergyman would now discontinue his weekly donation of bread; but he was greatly mistaken, for the pastor had hitherto given the bread to Marx, not on account of his virtue, but of his hunger.

CHAPTER VII.

HOW ROGUES DEAL WITH ONE ANOTHER.

It was evening before the Bailiff had completed his list of visits, and when he reached home, he found his tables filled almost as full as usual with a swaggering, tippling, good-for-nothing crowd of peasants. "Well, my good friends," he cried, well pleased; "it is very handsome in you not to desert me!"

"We haven't had enough of you yet!" they shouted, drinking his health uproariously. The noise was so great that Hummel bade his wife close the shutters and put out the lights toward the street; then they transported everything into the back room, whence no sound could penetrate to the ears of the passer-by.

When Michael appeared, the Bailiff took the vacant seat by his side, and clapping him on the shoulder, exclaimed: "Do you belong among the sinners? Since your invitation to work on the church-wall, I thought you had suddenly grown as saintly as our butcher did, when he had to ring the bell for the sexton every noon for a week!"

"No, Bailiff, I am not so suddenly converted; but if I once begin, I am not likely to stop."

"I would like to be your father confessor, Michael!"

"But I wouldn't like to have you!"

"Why not?"

"Because you would double my score with your holy chalk, while I should want a father confessor who would forgive and remit sins, not mark them down against me."

"I can remit sins as well as any one, and have it often enough to do," said the Bailiff, beckoning his companion to a little table which stood apart in the corner, and adding in a lower tone: "It is lucky for you that you have come."

"I am in need of luck!" Michael replied.

"Well, if you will take the trouble, you can make money enough in your new position."

"How?"

"You must get into the mason's good graces, and appear very hungry and poor."

"That I can do without making believe."

"Then you must often give your supper to your children, so that people shall think your heart is as soft as melted butter; and your children must run after you barefoot and in rags."

"That's not so hard, either."

"And when you are the favorite out of all the ten, then your real work will begin, which is, to do everything in your power to bring the building into discredit, and make mischief between the workmen and the authorities."

"That will not be quite so easy," observed the peasant dubiously.

"But you will make money by it."

"Two thalers in advance, Sir Bailiff, if you please! Otherwise I refuse to enlist in this campaign."

After a vain attempt to resist this demand, the Bailiff yielded, whereupon Michael expressed his willingness to receive orders.

"I think some night you could easily break down the scaffolding, and smash in a couple of the church-windows at a single blow; of course ropes, and tools, and all such odds and ends, would disappear mysteriously."

"Of course," echoed Michael.

"And then on a dark night it would not be difficult to

carry all the planks down hill to the river, and start them on
a journey to Holland."

"Nothing could be simpler! And I will hang a white
shirt on a pole, in the middle of the churchyard, so that if
the watchman and neighbors hear any noise, they may see a
ghost, and keep out of the way."

"What an idea, Michael! But that is not all. If there
are any of Arner's drawings or plans lying about, you must
carry them off where nobody would think of looking for
them, and at night go and get them to light your fire with."

"Very well, Sir."

"Then you must try to bring it about that your honorable
companions in service shall take life easy and dawdle over
their work; and if Arner or any one comes from the Castle,
the disorder must be at its height. I think you understand
me now. But, Michael, the most important thing of all is
that you and I shall be enemies; so we will begin now.
Somebody might report how we held counsel together in this
corner."

"Very true, Sir."

"Drink a couple of glasses, and then I will pretend to
call you to account for some reckoning. You will contradict
me, there will be high words between us, and we will put
you out of doors."

This was soon accomplished without difficulty.

"Bring us wine!" cried the men presently to their hostess.
"Bailiff, we will drink on the strength of the coming harvest,
— a sheaf out of the tithe for a measure of wine."

"You will pay me very soon!" observed their host ironi-
cally.

"Not so soon," they answered, "but all the heavier
weight."

Before long, all tongues were loosened by the wine, and
there arose from every table a mixture of curses and oaths,

of swaggering abuse and wanton jest. Stories were told of
theft and trickery, of lawsuits and riots, and of old Uli, who
had paid the penalty of his roguery on the gallows. They
were in the midst of this thrilling tale, when the Bailiff's
wife beckoned him to the door, and told him that Joseph
wanted to see him. She had made the fellow take off his
shoes and follow her noiselessly into a private room below,
where he was soon joined by the Bailiff, who accosted
him with : " What do you want so late, Joseph ? "

" Not much. I only wanted to tell you that it is all right
about the stone."

" I am glad to hear it, Joseph."

" My master was talking about the wall to-day, and said
the flint-stone close by was very good. But I told him to
his face that he was a fool, and that if the wall were made
of Schwendi stone, it would be as smooth as a plate. He
said nothing against it, so we shall open the quarry on
Monday, after the workmen have returned from the Castle."

" That is famous ! — if it were only done ! Your reward
is ready, Joseph."

" I am in great need of it at this very moment, Bailiff."

" Come for it Monday, after you have begun on the
quarry."

" But I wanted to go after my new boots to-morrow, —
give me three thalers now on our bargain ! "

" I can't very well at present. Come Monday evening."

But Joseph was firm. It was plain, he said, how much
confidence the Bailiff had in his word ; and when once the
quarry was opened, he felt sure that he, for his own part,
could no longer rely on the Bailiff's promises. All Hummel's
assurances were in vain, and he finally bade his wife give
Joseph three thalers. She took him aside, and earnestly
besought him to reconsider. " Don't be so foolish ! " she
pleaded. " You have been drinking, and will repent to·
morrow."

He insisted, however, and as he placed the money in Joseph's hand, he said once more: " You will not deceive me? "

" Heaven forbid! What do you take me for? " was the reply. But as he reached the door, Joseph muttered to himself: " Now I have my reward safer than it would have been in the Bailiff's chest. He is an old rogue, and can't make a fool of me. My master can take flint or blue stone now, for aught I care ! "

CHAPTER VIII.

GERTRUDE, meanwhile, was at home alone with her children. Thoughtful and silent, she prepared the supper, and
then took from the chest the Sunday clothes of all the
family, so that on the morrow no petty cares might distract
her thoughts from better things. When all was ready, she
gathered the children about her, for it was her custom every
Saturday to call their attention to their faults, and inculcate
any lessons which the events of the week might bring home
to their minds. To-day she was especially anxious to
impress their young hearts with a sense of the goodness of
God, as manifested during the past week; and when the
little hands were all folded, Gertrude thus spoke: "Children,
I have something joyful to tell you. Your dear father has
the promise of such good work that he will be able to
earn much more than before, and we may hope in future
to have less trouble and anxiety about getting our daily
bread. Thank the dear God, my children, for being so good
to us, and do not forget the time when every mouthful of
bread had to be counted! Think always of those who suffer
from hunger and want, as you did once, and if you have a
trifle more than you really need, do not grudge giving it to
them. Will you do this, children?"

"Oh, yes indeed, mother!" they all cried with one voice.
Gertrude now asked the children whether they would not
sometimes like to give away their afternoon bread to those
poorer than themselves, and on meeting with an eager

response, she told each one to think of some hungry child who might be gladdened by the gift. Nicholas mentioned their neighbor, little Rudy ; Lizzie spoke of Marx's daughter Betty ; and so with the others in turn. They were all so full of the idea that they resolved, with one accord, to carry out the plan on the following day.

Then Gertrude spoke of Arner's presents to the children, and promising to show them the money after their evening prayer, she began : " Well, my dears, how has it been about doing right this week?" The children looked at each other, and were silent. " Annie, have you been good this week?"

Casting down her eyes in shame, the child replied : " No, mother ; you know how it was with my little brother "—

" Annie, something might have happened to the child, — and just think how *you* would like it, if you should be shut up in a room all alone without food or amusement! Little children who are left alone in that way sometimes scream so that they injure themselves for life. Why, Annie, I could never feel easy about going away from home, if I thought you would not take good care of the child."

" Indeed, mother, I will never leave him alone again ! "

" And, Nicholas," said Gertrude, turning to her oldest son ; " how is it with you this week?"

" I don't remember anything wrong."

" Have you forgotten that you knocked down little Peggy. on Monday?"

" I didn't mean to, mother."

" I should hope not, Nicholas ! Aren't you ashamed of talking so? If you grow up without considering the comfort of those about you, you will have to learn the lesson through bitter experience. Remember that, and be careful, my dear boy.— And Lizzie, how have you behaved this week?"

" I can't think of anything out of the way this week, mother."

"Are you sure?"

"I really can't, mother, think as hard as I can; if I could, I would willingly tell you of it, mother."

"How you do manage to use as many words, even when you have nothing to say, as any one else who says a great deal!"

"What did I say now, mother?"

"Nothing at all, and yet a great deal. It is just what we have told you a thousand times, — you never think beforehand of what you are going to say, and yet must be always talking. What business was it of yours to tell the Bailiff, day before yesterday, that you knew Arner would come soon? Suppose your father had not wished him to know that he knew it, and your chattering had brought him into trouble?"

"I should be very sorry, mother. But neither of you said a word about its being a secret."

"Very well, I will tell your father when he comes home, that, whenever we are talking together, we must take care to add after each sentence: 'Lizzie may tell that to the neighbors, and talk about it at the well; but this she must not mention outside the house.' So then you will know precisely what you may chatter about."

"O mother, forgive me! That was not what I meant."

Gertrude talked similarly with all the other children about their faults, even saying to little Peggy: "You mustn't be so impatient for your soup, or I shall make you wait longer another time, and give it to one of the others."

After this was over, the children folded their hands and said their usual evening prayer, followed by a special prayer for Saturday night, which Gertrude had taught them. When the mother had uttered a final benediction, all sat quiet for a little while, until Lizzie broke the silence. "Now will you show us the new money, mother?"

" Yes. But, Lizzie, you are always the first to speak ! "
Nicholas sprang from his seat, and in pressing forward to
the light, gave little Peggy such a violent push that she cried
aloud.

" Nicholas ! " said his mother, " that is not right. It is
not a quarter of an hour since you promised to be more careful. You are not in earnest."

" O mother, I never will do so again as long as I live ! I
am really in earnest, and very sorry."

" So am I, dear boy ; but you will forget it all unless I
punish you. You must go to bed without your supper."

She led the boy to his room, while the other children stood
sadly by. " Do let him out again, just this once ! " they
entreated.

" No, my dears ; he must be cured of his carelessness."

" Then we'll not look at our money till to-morrow, so that
he can see it with us," proposed Annie.

" That is right, Annie ! " — and after giving the children
their supper, Gertrude went with them to the bedroom, where
Nicholas was still crying. " My dear, dear boy," she said,
" do be careful another time ! "

" Forgive me, dear mother ! " he cried, throwing his arms
about her neck. " Only forgive me and kiss me, and I don't
mind losing my supper at all."

Gertrude kissed him, and a warm tear fell upon his face.
She blessed the other children, and returned alone to the
dimly lighted room. A solemn stillness filled her heart ; she
was penetrated with a consciousness of God's goodness, and
the happiness of those who place their trust in him. She
was so deeply moved that she sank upon her knees and wept.
Her eyes were still moist when her husband returned home.
" Why are you weeping, Gertrude ? " he inquired.

" My dear husband, these are no tears of sorrow ; I
wanted to thank God for the blessings of this week, but my
heart was so full that I could not speak for weeping."

Leonard leaned his head upon her breast, and his eyes
were also filled with tears. Neither spoke for a short time ;
but at last Gertrude asked if he did not wish any supper.
" No," he replied ; " my heart is too full ; I cannot eat."
" Neither can I, dear. But I will tell you what we will
do. We will carry our supper to poor Rudy, whose mother
died to-day."

When they reached the house, Rudy was sitting weeping
beside the corpse, and his little boy called from the adjoining room, begging for bread, or raw roots, or anything
to eat. "Alas! I have nothing," answered the father.
" For Heaven's sake, be quiet till morning ! "

" But I am so hungry, father ! " moaned the child. " I
am so hungry I cannot sleep."

Leonard and Gertrude heard the words, and opening the
door, set down the food, and bade them eat quickly, before
it was cold. Deeply affected, the mourner called to the boy :
" Rudy, these are the people from whom you stole potatoes,
— and alas ! I too, have eaten some ! "

" Say no more about that," said Gertrude, " but eat."

" Do let us eat, father ! " begged the child.

" Well, then, say your grace."

The boy obeyed, then took up the spoon, trembled, wept
and ate. They put aside a part of the food for the sleeping
children, and the afflicted father attempted once more to
thank his benefactors. As he did so, a sigh escaped him.

" Is anything the matter, Rudy? Is there anything we
can do for you? " asked Leonard and Gertrude.

" No, nothing, thank you," he replied, with difficulty
repressing another deep sigh.

The two looked at him compassionately.   " But you sigh;
you certainly have some trouble at heart."

" Do tell them, father, they are so good ! " besought little
Rudy.

" May I? " said the poor man reluctantly. " I have neither shoes nor stockings, and to-morrow I must follow my mother to the grave, and the day after go to the Castle."

" The idea of tormenting yourself so about that ! " cried Leonard. " Why didn't you say so at first? I shall be very glad to provide you with them."

" And can you believe," said Rudy humbly, " that, after all that has happened, I will return them to you uninjured and with thanks? "

" Hush, Rudy ! I would trust you yet further than that. Your poverty and distress have made you too distrustful."

As Gertrude expressed a wish to look upon the dead, they all went with a feeble light to the bedside, and stood with tears in their eyes, gazing down upon the peaceful face. Then they covered up the lifeless form, and took leave of each other warmly, although without words.

CHAPTER IX.

TWO SERMONS, AND THEIR RESULTS.

THE next morning, the pastor preached a stirring sermon against the ungodly, who grow rich by oppressing and cheating the poor, and whose consciences never give them a moment's genuine peace. What right have such monsters of iniquity to present themselves before the table of the Lord? He closed with an exhortation to the poor and oppressed not to fear their powerful enemies, but to put their trust in the God of love, and to approach his holy meal with thanksgiving. The communion followed, in the distribution of which the Bailiff assisted, although at heart he was furious at the transparent allusions the clergyman's discourse contained. Hummel went home and summoned his good-for-nothing comrades to the house, who joined him in abusing the sermon. But it happened that a church-warden, who lived in the same street with the Bailiff, and saw the men slink into the tavern between the services, set a reliable man to watch and see whether the fellows came out again before the afternoon meeting. As they did not, he went to the pastor, and informed him of his discovery.

When the good man was reading to his congregation that afternoon the story of the Passion, he came to the words: "And when Judas had taken the sop, Satan entered into his heart;" and he proceeded to discourse at length upon the history of the traitor. He declared that all those who went from the communion-table to gambling and drinking were not one whit better than Judas himself, and would come to the same end. He even grew so excited that he brought his fist down with violence upon the pulpit-rail, which he had not done for many years. The people at first were astonished, but soon began to suspect the cause of this unusual zeal; and before long, every eye was turned to the unfortunate wife of the Bailiff, who sat beside his empty seat. She dared not look any one in the face, and escaped from the church during the singing, followed by whispered jeers. She ran home as fast as she could, entered the room, flung her prayer-book angrily into the midst of the flasks and glasses, and began to sob aloud.

"What is the matter?" cried the Bailiff and the neighbors.

"That you ought to know without asking! It isn't right for you to be tippling here on a Sunday!"

"Is *that* all?" inquired the Bailiff.

"This is the first time you ever cried about it," sneered the peasants.

"I thought at the very least you had lost your purse," said her husband. "Leave off blubbering and tell us what the matter is!"

"The pastor must have learned that these friends of yours were drinking here during the sermon."

"What Satan can have told him that?" exclaimed the Bailiff in dismay.

"What Satan, you fool? They didn't come down the chimney, did they? — but walked calmly along the street with their tobacco-pipes, past the churchwarden's house. And now the parson has been talking in a way I cannot describe, and all the people pointed at me with their fingers. — But, neighbors, go as quickly as ever you can, out through the back door, before they have finished singing, so that, as they come home from church, they will find each one of you at his own door."

"Yes, go!" ordered the Bailiff.

When they were alone, his wife told him in detail of the
pastor's sermon, which so terrified him that for a time he
was unable to speak. When he had somewhat recovered,
he told her how furious he had been over the morning's discourse. " I could not pray at communion," he said. " My
heart was like a stone, and when the pastor gave me the
bread, he looked at me in a way I shall never forget. A
cold perspiration stood out on my forehead as I took the
bread from him, and I trembled so at the altar that I could
hardly hold the goblet. Joseph came up in his torn boots,
and cast down his rascally eyes when he saw me, — how I
shuddered at the thought of my three thalers! Next came
Gertrude, raised her eyes toward heaven, and fixed them on
the cup, as if she did not see me. She hates me, and seeks
my ruin; yet she behaved as if I were not there. Then the
mason approached, and looked at me as sorrowfully as if he
wanted to ask my forgiveness from the bottom of his heart,
whereas he would be glad to bring me to the gallows if he
could. Finally Michael came, as pale and terrified as I
myself. I was afraid Hans Wust would be the next, and if
he had come, I should certainly have sunk to the ground.
As it was, when I went back to my seat, I trembled so from
head to foot that I could not hold the singing-book. And
all the time I kept thinking: 'Arner is to blame for every
thing.' And in my anger and rage something came into my
head which I hardly dare tell you, — I thought of digging
up the great boundary stone on the mountain, and rolling it
down the precipice; nobody knows of this stone except
myself, and if it were removed, Arner would lose a third
part of his forest territory, for the government boundary
would cut away the piece of land in a straight line from the
rest of his property."

Terrified by her husband's words, the Bailiff's wife earnestly exhorted him to give up all intercourse with his

evil companions, who would be the ruin of him, she said, before long. He made no reply, but walked out absently into the garden, and made a restless tour of his premises, ever accompanied by the strange thought which possessed his mind. The upshot of his reflections was that he dared not remove the boundary ; for the task must be performed at night, when he had not courage to go up into the dark wood alone, for fear of ghosts and hobgoblins. Yet he could not banish the idea, and to deliver himself from his own thoughts, he ran out into the street, and engaged in conversation with the first neighbor he met. Later he found a couple of thirsty wretches, whom he brought into the house ; and by treating them to liquor, he induced them to bear him company for the remainder of this dreadful day.

CHAPTER X.

SUNDAY JOYS AND CHILDISH CHARACTER.

MEANWHILE, the Sunday had been very differently spent in the humble dwelling of the mason. While Leonard and Gertrude were at church, the children prayed, sang, and reviewed what they had learned during the week, so as to be ready to repeat it to their mother in the evening. Lizzie, the oldest, had the care of baby Peggy during Gertrude's absence, and it was her greatest delight to dress, feed, and tend the little one. It was pretty to see her motherly airs as she dandled and kissed and played with her charge. How pleased she was when the baby laughed back at her with outstretched arms, and kicked with its tiny feet! Then it would grasp Lizzie's cap, or her pig-tails, or her nose, and crow over her bright Sunday neckerchief, until Nicholas and Annie would come up behind and crow in imitation; then the little one would turn at the sound, and laugh at the merry Nicholas, who would spring forward to kiss his baby sister. This would arouse Lizzie's jealousy, and she would exert herself to the utmost to make the little darling laugh at her. She devoted herself to the amusement of her charge, lifting the child in her arms almost to the ceiling, and then letting it down carefully to the very ground, until it screamed aloud with delight. Then she would hold it close to the looking-glass, so that it laughed at the baby within; but the most joyful moment of all was when the little one espied its mother far down the street, crowed, stretched out its tiny hands, and nearly sprang out of Lizzie's arms.

Gertrude was satisfied with her children to-day, for they had done everything as she had told them. They now had their reward in a frolic with their parents, for climbing joyfully into the laps of father and mother, the children possessed themselves of their hands, and clasped their necks tightly with small arms. Ever since Gertrude had been a mother, this was her Sunday delight; but to-day Leonard's eyes filled with tears at the thought that he had often deprived himself of these home joys. The happy parents talked with the children of their Father in heaven, and the sufferings of their Saviour, while the little ones listened attentively. The noon hour passed as swiftly and happily as a wedding feast, and the peal of bells again summoned Leonard and Gertrude to church.

When they returned home in the afternoon, the children ran down the steps to meet them, crying: " Oh, do hurry, mother! We want to repeat what we have learned this week, and get through as soon as possible."

" Why are you in such desperate haste, my dears? " asked Gertrude smiling.

" Why, when we are through, mother, you know what you promised us yesterday about the bread. We may, mother, mayn't we? "

" First I will see how well you know what you have learned," was the reply.

The lesson was soon satisfactorily concluded, whereupon Gertrude brought out the bread, and two dishes of milk from which she had not removed the cream, because it was a holiday. Not one of the children touched the bread, but each rejoiced over his or her piece, maintaining that it was the largest. When the milk had disappeared, Nicholas crept up to his mother's side, and taking her hand, whispered: "You will give me just one mouthful of bread for myself, will you not, mother? "

" You have your piece, Nicholas."

" But I must give it to Rudy."

" I haven't told you to give it to him," said his mother. " You can eat it if you like."

" I don't want to eat it; but you will give me just one mouthful? "

" Certainly not, my boy."

" Why not? "

" So that you needn't imagine we are only to think of the poor after our own hunger is satisfied. And now will you give him the whole of it? "

" Yes, mother, every bit. I know he is frightfully hungry, and we have supper at six."

" Yes, Nicholas, and I hardly think he will have anything to eat then."

The mother now turned to the other children, and asked if they, too, had quite decided to give their bread away, receiving in each case an affirmative answer. " That is right, children," she said. " But now, how will you set about it? — Nicholas, how are you going to manage with your bread? "

" I'll run as fast as I can, and call Rudy. I shall not put it in my pocket, so that he may have it all the quicker. Let me go, mother! "

" Stop a minute, Nicholas! — Lizzie, what are you going to do? "

" I am not going to do like Nicholas. I shall call Betty into a corner, and hide the bread under my apron, so that nobody will see it, not even her father."

" And Annie? "

" I can't tell where I shall find Harry — I shall give it to him just as it happens."

" And Jonas, you little rogue, you have some mischief in your head; how are you planning to do it? "

" I shall stick my bread into his mouth, mother, as you do

to me in fun. ' Open your mouth and shut your eyes,' I shall say, and then put it between his teeth. Don't you think he'll laugh?"

" That is all very well, children," said Gertrude. " But I must tell you one thing : you must give away the bread quietly, so no one may see, that people needn't think you want to show off your generosity."

" Whew! mother," cried Nicholas ; " then I must put my bread in my pocket? "

" Of course, Nicholas."

" That is just what occurred to me, mother," said Lizzie. " You know I said just now that I wouldn't do like him."

" You are always the wisest, Lizzie. I forgot to praise you for it, and you do well to remind me of it yourself." Lizzie colored, and was silent.

The children departed on their several missions. Nicholas ran at full speed to Rudy's cottage, but no one was in sight. After calling several times without any reply, he went into the house. Little Rudy was sitting with his father and the other children, weeping beside the coffin of his grandmother, when Nicholas opened the door of the room, and started back at sight of the dead. The father saw him, and thinking there might be some message from Leonard, ran after the boy, and asked what he wanted. " Nothing," answered Nicholas ; " I only wanted to see Rudy, but he is praying now."

" Come in, if you want to see him."

" I can't. Please let him come out to me a minute ! "

The father beckoned to his son, but little Rudy called out to his friend : " I don't want to come into the street now, Nicholas ! I would rather stay with my grandmother, — they will take her away from me soon."

" Just come a minute ! " pleaded the visitor.

He came out ; and Nicholas, taking him by the arm, whispered mysteriously: "Come, I have something to say to you!" and leading him into a retired corner, he transferred the bread from his own pocket to Rudy's, and ran away as quickly as he had come.

Lizzie, meanwhile, had advanced with measured pace to the upper village, where Marx's daughter Betty lived. The latter was standing at the window, and slipped quietly out of the room in response to a signal from her friend. Not so quietly, however, but that her father noticed it, and creeping after her, concealed himself behind the door.

"Here, Betty, I have some bread for you," began Lizzie.

The girl stretched out a trembling hand for the offered food, as she answered: "How good you are, Lizzie! I am very hungry. But why should you bring me bread now?"

"Because I am fond of you, Betty. We have enough bread now; my father is to build the church."

"So is mine."

"Yes, but yours is only a day-laborer."

"That is all the same, if we only get bread by it."

"Have you had to suffer much from hunger, Betty?"

"Oh, I only hope the worst is over!"

"What did you have for dinner to-day?" inquired her guest.

"That I mustn't tell you."

"Why not?"

"If my father should know I told you, he would "—

"I should be likely to go straight and tell him!" observed Lizzie in an injured tone. Betty drew from her pocket a piece of raw turnip.

"Goodness!" ejaculated her visitor; "nothing but that?"

"No, not for the last two days."

"And you mustn't tell anybody, or ask for anything from any one?"

" No, indeed! If he knew what I have told you, I should have a hard time of it."

" Eat your bread before you have to go in," advised her friend prudently.

Betty was not slow to follow this counsel, but had no sooner taken a bite than the pious Marx opened the door, and said : " What are you eating, my child? "

The unfortunate girl gulped down the unchewed mouthful, and answered : " Nothing, father."

" Nothing? Just you wait!— And, Lizzie, it is no favor to me to give my children bread behind my back, so that they shall tell such outrageous lies about what we eat and drink in, the house. —You wretched Betty! Didn't we have an omelette for dinner? "

Lizzie, at this juncture, hastened away as rapidly as she had come deliberately, while the affectionate father seized his daughter by the arm, and dragged her into the house, whence Lizzie heard cries issuing long after she had left it far behind.

Annie found Harry at his door, and gave him her piece of bread without further adventures.

Little Jonas crept around Michael's house, until Bobby saw him, and came out. " What are you after, Jonas? " he cried.

" I want to have some fun."

" All right, come on ! "

" Will you do just as I say, Bobby? If you will, we shall have lots of fun."

" Well, then, what shall we do? "

" You must open your mouth and shut your eyes."

" Yes, and then you'll put something dirty in my mouth."

" No, Bobby, I won't, — on my honor ! "

" Well, then. But look out and don't cheat me ! " — opening his mouth and half shutting his eyes.

" Shut your eyes tight, or it's no fair ! "

The little fellow obeyed, and Jonas quickly put the bread between his teeth, and ran away.

" This *is* fun ! " said Bobby, sitting down on the door-step to enjoy the feast.

His father Michael had observed the children's play from the window, and recognized Leonard's little Jonas. His heart smote him as he thought of the treacherous part he had been about to play towards the mason ; and he resolved upon the spot to have nothing more to do with the evil designs of the Bailiff.

CHAPTER XI.

THE BAILIFF GROWS STILL MORE ANGRY.

LEONARD was awakened the next morning by a voice outside his window. It was Flink, the armed servant from the Castle, with orders that the mason should have the men begin to break the stones that morning. Leonard remembered he had heard something about the workmen going to the Castle to thank Arner, but hoped it was early enough to anticipate this manœuvre. To his annoyance, however, he found that the men had started half an hour ago. Flink hastened to a high hill, commanding the road; but although he shouted until he was hoarse, it was of no avail, and the dimly discernible figures had soon vanished in the distance. The Bailiff, however, who had started later than the others, heard the cries, and turned back to ascertain their cause. Great was his vexation when Flink informed him that in consequence of a severe headache the night before, he had delayed the delivery of his message until morning. "You cursed scoundrel! what kind of a trick do you call that?" thundered the Bailiff.

"It may not be so bad, after all," returned the man. "How the Devil was I to know that the fellows would all go capering out of the village before daybreak? Was it by your orders?"

"Yes, you dog, it was. And now I suppose I shall have to pay for your fault!"

"I shall not have any too easy a time of it myself," said Flink ruefully.

The Bailiff advised the unlucky messenger to throw himself on Leonard's mercy, and beg the mason to tell Arner he
had received the message on Sunday, but that as it was
a holiday, he had put off telling the men until the morrow.
Flink acted on this suggestion, and the good-natured mason
made no objection. When he consulted his wife, however,
Gertrude said: "I am afraid of everything which is not
straightforward. If Arner asks you about it, you must tell
him the truth; but if, as is probable, no one inquires about
the matter, you can let it rest as they wish, since it will
injure nobody." And thus it was settled.

Meanwhile, the workmen reached the Castle, and were at
once admitted to the presence of Arner, who asked them
kindly what they wanted. When they had managed to stammer their thanks, Arner inquired at whose bidding they had
come, and on learning the truth, dismissed them, saying:
"This has occurred contrary to my wishes. But go now, in
God's name, and if you are faithful and industrious, I shall
be glad if the work benefits any of you. Tell your master
to begin breaking the stones to-day."

On their way back, the men talked of the kindness of
Arner, which they could not but contrast unfavorably with
the Bailiff's treatment. "What a mean trick it was, to lead
us such a dance without orders, and then leave us in the
lurch!" cried one.

"That is his way," remarked another.

"It's a mean way, then," responded Leuk, the man who
had first spoken.

"Yes, but the Bailiff is a worthy man, and the like of us
can't always see all sides of the question!" said Kriecher as
loud as he could, — for he saw the Bailiff stealthily advancing toward them in the hollow.

"The Devil! *You* can praise him, if you like, but *I* shall
praise Arner!" shouted Leuk, who did not observe Hummel's
approach.

The Bailiff now appeared from the neighboring hedge, and after greeting his neighbors, asked Leuk why he was sounding Arner's praises so loudly.

"We were only saying how good-natured and kind he was," answered the man in some confusion.

"But that was not all," said the Bailiff.

"All that I know of," returned Leuk doggedly.

"It isn't very nice in a man to deny his words in that way, Leuk," remarked Kriecher. "And he was not the only one, Sir Bailiff. Several of them were complaining that you had left them in the lurch, but I told them that such as we couldn't expect to know your Honor's reasons. Then Leuk told me I might praise the Bailiff, but he would praise Arner."

The men here began to shake their heads, and murmur against Kriecher, so that the Bailiff, pressing the hand of his hypocritical ally, made haste to change the subject, and asked whether Arner had been angry. "Not at all," replied the men; "he only told us to hurry home and begin our work without delay."

"Tell the mason so, and that the misunderstanding is of no consequence," said Hummel, as he left them and continued on his way.

When the Bailiff reached the Castle, Arner kept him waiting for some time ; and when the nobleman finally appeared, he asked Hummel in some displeasure why he had taken it upon himself to counsel the masons to come to the Castle that morning.

"I thought it my duty," replied the Bailiff, "to advise the men to thank your Grace for the work."

"Your duty is to do what is useful to me and my people, and what I bid you ; but not to send poor men on a wild-goose chase, and teach them to make fine speeches, which are as useless as they are undesired. — But I sent for you in order to tell you that I will no longer suffer the offices of

bailiff and tavern-keeper to be united in the same person. I
will give you your choice between the two, and desire to
know your decision a fortnight from to-day."

The Bailiff was so thunderstruck by the suddenness of the
announcement, that he was hardly able to stammer his humble thanks for the two weeks' respite, and left his chief soon
after in a transport of anger and despair. He stopped under
the old nut-tree by the road, to take breath and collect his
scattered senses. He was so weak that he could hardly
think, and taking his brandy-bottle from his pocket, he
gulped down a half pint at one draught. It revived his
strength immediately, and all his old pride returned, so that
he responded to the greetings of the passers-by with a
haughty nod, and carried his knotted stick with a commanding air, as if his power were greater in the land than that of
ten Arners.

On his way home, the Bailiff stopped at the tavern in
Hirzau, and drank and boasted among the assembled peasants. The old forester from the Castle stopped, in passing,
for a glass, and Hummel, who dreaded being alone, proposed
that they should walk back to the village together. On the
way he inquired of his companion whether there were ghosts
in the forest at night. " Why do you ask me that?" queried
the forester.

" Because I want to know."

" You are an old fool! The idea of being Bailiff thirty
years, and then asking such absurd questions! — But I'll help
you out of your uncertainty, if you'll pay me with a bottle of
wine."

" Two, if you can succeed in convincing me! "

" Well, I have been forester forty years, and ever since I
was four years old, I was brought up in the woods by my
father. As it would not do for a forester to believe in ghosts
or hobgoblins, he used to take me into the forest on dark

nights, and then whenever he saw a light or heard a noise, we hurried after it, over stumps and ditches, through swamps and bushes. It always turned out to be tramps or thieves, who took to their heels when he shouted: 'Away, rogues!' And sometimes the wild beasts make queer noises, and the rotten tree-trunks give out light. That is all I have ever found in the forest; but it is greatly to my advantage for my neighbors to believe in ghosts, so that I need not turn out on dark nights after the rascals."

Here the forester entered a by-path which led into the wood, while the Bailiff went on, busied with his own reflections, until he reached the confines of the village, where he beheld the masons at work on the great stones which lay about on the plain. " I cannot go by that accursed Joseph in silence!" he exclaimed to himself. He sat down upon the hillside, on which the last rays of the setting sun were falling, and waited until the village bell rang out six o'clock ; then the masons started on their homeward way, and the Bailiff followed them.

CHAPTER XII.

RATS DESERT A SINKING SHIP, AND THE DEVIL APPEARS TO THE INHABITANTS OF BONNAL.

AFTER Hans Wüst had parted from the Bailiff on Saturday night, he was so overcome with remorse for his perjury that he was almost beside himself. He rolled on the floor, tore his hair, and struck himself violently with his fists. The following day he could neither eat nor drink, but wandered about, groaning in agony of spirit, until at night, exhausted by his anguish, he at last fell asleep. He awoke with the resolution not to bear his distress longer alone, and making a bundle of his Sunday coat and whatever else he could find, he went to the pastor's house. The good man noticed the wild looks of his approaching guest, and going to meet him, asked what was the matter, inviting him so kindly into his room, that poor Wüst was reässured, and made a clean breast of the whole matter. The pastor assured him of forgiveness from above, and persuaded him that the only right and wise course was to confess all to Arner. The poor wretch was melted to tears by the parson's comforting words. and finally took courage to make a request. He told his counsellor of the eight florins which he owed the Bailiff, and tendered his bundle of belongings as security for the advancement of the money. The good pastor immediately offered him the sum as a loan, insisting that the Sunday coat should be carried home again. Once more light at heart, Wüst hastened to the Bailiff's house, and as the latter was not at home, gave the money to his wife, who received and counted it in no small wonder and perturbation of spirit.

Before night, another of the Bailiff's tools had deserted him. On this, the first day the workmen were together, Leonard won the hearts of all the men by his patience with their stupidity, and his good-natured zeal in undertaking the hardest and most disagreeable parts of the labor himself. Michael, while working by the master's side the whole afternoon, strengthened himself in the resolution he had made the evening before, and at night proposed to accompany Leonard home, saying that he had something to tell him. Arrived at the mason's cottage, he related the rogue's business in which the Bailiff had sought to enlist him, and confessed that he had already received two thalers in advance on the bargain. Leonard and Gertrude were overcome with horror. He exhorted them to make their minds easy on his account, and proposed to lay a trap for the Bailiff, by pretending to be true to his agreement, and on the next day transferring some of the tools to the Bailiff's house, which should then be searched by a warrant from Arner. But the mason and his wife would not consent to this. "We ought to thank God," said Gertrude, "that we are delivered from the danger which threatened us; but it is not for us to take vengeance on our enemies." Michael owned that she was right, but confessed that he had already spent a half thaler of his bribe, so that it would be impossible for him to restore the whole amount at present. Leonard gladly advanced the money out of Michael's future wages, and the latter left his new friends, bent on freeing himself at once from all obligation to Hummel.

When the Bailiff reached home, he found his wife alone, so that he could give vent at last to the accumulated rage of the day. The terrified woman tried in vain to check his violence. "Haven't I reason to be angry?" he burst forth

"Arner is going to take away either my license or my Bailiff's mantle in a fortnight."

"I know it," she said; "although I did not learn it until this evening. The whole village knows it by this time. And something else has happened,—Hans Wüst has brought back the eight florins."

Thunderstruck at these words, the Bailiff gazed stupidly at his wife without speaking. Finally he asked her for the money, and she brought it in a broken beer-glass. He looked at it without counting it, and observed: "This doesn't come from the Castle, for Arner never gives such coin as this. If I had been here, I would have found out where it came from. — Bring me wine, wife!"

She placed the tankard before him, and pacing the room, he muttered between the draughts: "I must ruin the mason first of all. Michael must ruin him, if it costs me a hundred thalers!"

At this moment there was a knock at the door. "Who comes so late?" he cried with a start.

"Open the door, Bailiff!" called Michael's voice from without.

Hummel hastened to bid his visitor welcome. "What good news do you bring, Michael?"

"Not much. I only wanted to tell you" —

"Don't stand there in the street! Come in!"

"No, Bailiff, I must go home. I only wanted to say that I have repented of our bargain."

"Repented? Nonsense! No, Michael, that must not be. If two thalers are not enough, I'll give you more. Only come in!"

"No, Bailiff, on no account. There are your two thalers."

"I swear I will not take them from you! Don't be such a fool. but come in!"

Michael was forced to follow him, but as soon as he had entered the room, he laid the money on the table, and hastened away.

The Bailiff stood awhile speechless; his eyes rolled wildly, and he foamed at the mouth. At length he burst out: "Wife, bring me brandy! It must be, — I am going!"

"Oh, where are you going this pitch-dark night?" she cried in terror.

"I am going to dig up the stone, — give me the bottle!" — and deaf to all entreaties, he seized pickaxe, shovel and mattock, and hastened up the mountain in the darkness. Although emboldened by rage and brandy, yet whenever he saw a bit of incandescent wood, or heard the rustling of a hare near his path, he halted trembling for a moment, and then rushed madly on again; until at length he reached the solitary mile-stone, where he at once set vigorously to work. Ere long, he was startled by a noise, and looking up, saw a black figure emerge from the bushes and come toward him. Light shone around the apparition, and fire burned upon its head. "It is the Devil incarnate!" gasped the Bailiff, and with horrible cries he took to his heels, leaving tools, hat and brandy-bottle behind him. As he ran blindly on, a most unearthly sound of rattling and clanking continually pursued him, and he heard ever and anon a hollow voice, which seemed to curdle the blood in his veins, crying behind him: "Oh! Ah! Uh! Hummel! Wait, Bailiff, you are mine!"

The Bailiff rushed on toward the village, shouting at the top of his lungs: "Murder! Help! Watchman! The Devil is after me!" The watchman heard the cries and commotion, and was so terrified that he tapped on the neighbors' windows to summon them to his aid. When ten or a dozen were assembled, they proposed to sally forth with torches and fire-arms, in the direction of the noise, taking new

bread, a Testament and a Psalter in their pockets, to coun-
teract the power of the Devil. The men stopped first at the
Bailiff's house, to be certain that he was actually away from
home, and were joined by his wife, who was almost beside
herself with anxiety.

As they approached the scene of the hubbub, the hollow
voice and the clanking suddenly ceased. Kunz, who happened to be the foremost of the band, now came up and
seized the howling Bailiff roughly by the arm. "O Devil,
spare me!" screamed poor Hummel, still too much terrified
to use his eyes or ears. The rest of the men hung back, and
looked cautiously about with their torches, to see if any sign
of the Devil remained; but Kunz boldly declared it to be his
opinion that a poacher or a woodman had made game of them
all, since at his approach he had heard a man run up hill.
"And what is to prevent the Devil from running so as to be
heard?" asked the men, while all agreed that it was no
human voice which had so alarmed them, and that a whole
wagon-load of iron could not make as fearful a rattling as
the sound which had reached their ears.

The Bailiff heard none of the conversation, but when he
reached home, he begged the neighbors not to leave him, and
they willingly consented to remain in the tavern.

CHAPTER XIII.

THE CULPRIT CONFESSES AND RECEIVES HIS SENTENCE.

IN the mean time, the alarm had spread through the village, and the pastor, among others, received accounts of the awful catastrophe. Thinking he might turn the Bailiff's fright to good account, he betook himself to the tavern, and besought the neighbors, who rose and saluted him respectfully at his entrance, to leave him alone with Hummel for a while. As they departed, the good man cautioned them not to be in too great haste to talk about the affair, since at present it was impossible for any one to judge precisely what had really happened. But the men only grumbled outside the door: "He is always an old fool, and doesn't believe anything!"

When the pastor found himself alone with the Bailiff, he questioned him kindly about his strange adventure. "I am a poor unlucky wretch," was the reply, "and Satan himself tried to catch me."

"Did you actually see anybody?" inquired the clergyman.

"Yes, I saw him running toward me. He was a great black man with fire on his head, and he followed me to the foot of the mountain."

"Well, Bailiff, we will let the matter rest there, as it is impossible to explain it. And it is of no great consequence, after all, when you consider that there is an eternity, in which the unrighteous will surely fall into his clutches. It is *this* danger which, considering your age and your way of life, ought to cause you anxiety."

The poor Bailiff was wrought up to such a pitch of terror that he besought the pastor piteously to tell him how he might escape the Devil's power, and regain the grace of God. The good man counselled him to repentance, and restitution of his unlawfully acquired property. Hummel was so thoroughly cowed that he promised to restore Rudy's meadow, and on being questioned, confessed for what purpose he had ascended the mountain the previous night. After some further counsel on the part of his adviser, the unhappy man consented to throw himself on Arner's mercy, and confess everything.

After praying and talking awhile with the Bailiff, the pastor went home and wrote to Arner, telling him of Hans Wüst's disclosure of the day before, and its unexpected confirmation through the Bailiff's confession. Before this letter reached its destination, however, Arner had already become acquainted with the events of the preceding night from another source, as we shall learn presently. He wrote the pastor that he would come to Bonnal that very day, to hold a meeting about the boundary-stone, adding that it was his intention at the same time to enact a little comedy before the peasants, to cure them of their superstition. He would also bring his wife and children, he said, as they were anxious to be present at the comedy.

When he had finished this letter, Arner went to his stable, and from his fifty cows chose out the finest for Hübel-Rudy, and ordered it to be led to Bonnal to await his pleasure. Then he sat down and meditated awhile, earnestly and sadly, on the sentence he should pass on the Bailiff. After an early dinner, he set forth with his wife and children in the direction of the village. As they passed the laborers, who were busied in breaking stones, the nobleman descended from the carriage to inspect their work, and praised the good order and regularity which prevailed, in a way which convinced even the dullest among them that not the slightest neglect or irregularity would have escaped his notice.

When Arner reached the pastor's house, he sent immediately for young Meyer, whom he destined to fill the now vacant office of bailiff, and thus addressed him: " Meyer, I am on the point of dismissing my Bailiff; but despite his offences, I could yet wish that during his life-time he may continue to receive some portion of the revenue of his office. You are in comfortable circumstances, and if I make you Bailiff, I suppose you would be willing to allow the old man one hundred florins a year out of your salary." On receiving a submissive reply in the affirmative, Arner continued: " Now, Meyer, you must go with my secretary and the justice Aebi to the tavern, and seal up all Hummel's papers and accounts. You will have to keep a sharp look-out that none of the documents are secreted."

While the three men were fulfilling this order, the Bailiff's wife approached the blackboard with a wet sponge. Meyer stopped her, and had a copy made of the following, which was written on the board in chalk: " Saturday, the 18th, paid to Leonard's man Joseph, three thalers." The Bailiff and his wife refused at first to give any explanation regarding this entry, until the good pastor adjured Hummel not to aggravate the mischief by concealment, when he made a clean breast of the matter.

Arner had the Bailiff, Wüst and Joseph brought to the parsonage, and submitted to a legal examination. When their depositions had been taken down, he ordered the bells to be rung to summon the people to the square under the linden-tree, where the village meetings were held. Arner's wife Theresa and the pastor's wife, with the children and servants of both families, took up their position in the churchyard, which commanded a view of the square.

Arner first ordered the prisoners to be brought forth, and after they had read aloud the confessions they had previ-

ously made, he bade the Bailiff kneel down and receive his
sentence, which he pronounced as follows : "Unhappy man!
It grieves me to the heart to inflict upon you, in your old
age, the punishment which necessarily follows misdeeds like
yours. You have deserved death, not because Rudy's
meadow or my boundary-stone are worth a man's life, but
because a career of perjury and robbery can bring an
unlimited amount of danger and suffering upon a whole
community. Yet in consideration of your age, and of the
fact that a part of your offences were committed against me
personally, I have decided to spare your life. Your punishment shall be this : to-day, in company with all the overseers of the village, and whoever wishes to go beside, you
shall be carried to the boundary-stone, and in chains restore
everything to its former condition. Then you shall be
brought to the village jail, where for a fortnight the pastor
shall visit you daily, and receive from you a full account ot
your past career. Two weeks from Sunday he shall relate
from the pulpit the history of your life, with your domestic
troubles, your hard-heartedness, your contempt of oaths,
and your injustice to poor and rich alike ; and this must all
be confirmed by your own testimony. With this I would
gladly discharge you ; but since it is necessary, where there
are so many rude and unprincipled people, to set up an
example and a warning, I must add one more penalty ; to-
morrow morning the executioner shall lead you under the
gallows of Bonnal, and there bind your right hand to a stake,
and smear the first three fingers with an indelible black dye.
But it is my express desire that no one shall imbitter this
your hour of suffering by mockery or laughter, and that all
shall look on silently, with uncovered heads."

Arner then condemned Hans Wüst to eight days' im-
prisonment, while Joseph, as a stranger, he banished from
the territory, forbidding him to return, under penalty of
being sent to the House of Correction.

CHAPTER XIV.

A GHOSTLY COMEDY.

IT was now time for Arner's little game to begin, when to his surprise, the first move was made by the opposite party. The peasants had been greatly dissatisfied with the incredulity their pastor had manifested the night before, and the good man had also become obnoxious to the large landowners, ever since he had announced from the pulpit that it was wrong in them to oppose Arner's project of dividing a certain strip of meadow-land among the poor. Accordingly, a number of the citizens had held a council that morning, and as a result of their deliberations, the hypocrite and miser Hartknopf now arose in the assembly, and began: " Gracious Sir, is it allowable to bring forward an affair of conscience, in the name of the peasants of your faithful community of Bonnal?"

" I am ready to hear," Arner replied. " Who are you?"

" I am Jacob Christopher Frederic Hartknopf, churchwarden and elder of Bonnal, fifty-six years of age. And the overseers of the village have requested me, in the name of the community, to lay a statement before you, as they are not accustomed to speaking upon spiritual subjects."

" Well, Mr Hartknopf, to the point!" cried Arner impatiently.

" Gracious Sir, we have inherited from our ancestors a belief that the Devil and his spirits often appear to men ; and since now it has become evident that our old belief in spirits is true (as none of us ever doubted for a moment),

we felt we must take the liberty of informing our gracious
master that our reverend pastor, God forgive him, is not of
this belief. We know very well that your Grace is of the
same opinion as the pastor regarding spirits; but since in
matters of belief we must obey God rather than man, we
hope your Grace will pardon us, if we humbly beg that
in future our reverend pastor may teach our children from
the stand-point of our old belief, and not talk any more
against spirits, in which we are bound to believe. And we
would request that a Sunday may be set apart before long,
as a day of fasting and prayer, that we may do penance in
sackcloth and ashes for the increasing sin of disbelief in
spirits."

Arner and the parson could hardly repress their laughter
until he had finished, but many of the peasants sprang to
their feet, crying: "Gracious master! We all agree with
what the church-warden has said."

Arner, however, put on his hat, and looking seriously
around, said: "Neighbors, there was no need of any orator
for such folly as this! The whole affair, with the appearance of the Devil, rests upon error, and you ought to be
ashamed to insult your wise and excellent pastor through
such a wretched fellow as your church-warden!"

"But it is plain that the Devil appeared to the Bailiff
last night, and tried to catch him," broke in the peasants
eagerly.

"You are laboring under a mistake, neighbors," returned
Arner; "and before supper-time you will blush for your
stupidity."

"But, Sir," they cried, "we all heard the dreadful voice
of Satan himself!"

"I know very well that you heard shouts, accompanied by
a bellowing and clanking. But how can you say certainly
that it was the Devil? Might it not have been that one or
more men took a fancy to frighten the Bailiff?"

This suggestion was indignantly repelled. "Not ten, no, not twenty men all together, could have made such a noise; and if you had been there, gracious Sir, it never would have entered your head that it could be men at all."

"But, neighbors," persisted Arner; "darkness is deceptive, and when we are once startled, we see and hear everything double. I am quite certain that you are mistaken."

"No, gracious Sir, there is no possibility of that."

"I am almost inclined to think I could convince you of your error."

"Your Grace is joking!" they all cried.

"No, I am not joking. If you will agree to divide the common, I will keep my word, and convince you that all the roaring and rattling was made by one man. Will you take the risk?"

"Yes, Sir, that we will! If you will do what you say, and prove to our entire satisfaction that it was one man who made all the noise we heard last night, we will agree to divide the common; but otherwise not."

Arner hereupon drew a large white handkerchief ostentatiously from his pocket, and a few moments after, amid a peal of laughter from the churchyard, a tall stranger was seen approaching, armed with a dark basket and a lantern. "What fool is this, who walks about in broad daylight with a lighted lantern?" asked the peasants.

"It is my poulterer from Arnheim," replied Arner. "Ho, Christopher! What do you want here?"

"I have a story to tell, gracious Sir."

On receiving permission to proceed, the poulterer set down his basket, and began as follows: "Gracious Sir, reverend pastor, and neighbors! Here are the pickaxe, the mattock, the spade, the brandy-bottle, the tobacco-pipe and the felt hat of your worthy Bailiff, which he left near the boundary-stone in his flight, when I drove him away from his fine job early this morning, and chased him down the mountain."

"And are we to believe," asked the peasants, "that it was you who made all the noise? Master, this proof is not sufficient; we ask for another."

"Just wait a moment!" said Arner. "He has a lantern with him, and perhaps will be able to enlighten you a little. Only please be silent until he has done speaking."

The men obeyed, and the poulterer continued: "Why are you not civil enough to let me finish? If you don't listen to me, you will never hear the last of it, for there is not a syllable of truth in the Devil's having appeared to the Bailiff. It was I who frightened him, — I, the poulterer, just as I stand here, with this basket, with a new black goat-skin stretched over it, because it rained yesterday morning. And I had this lantern hung to my basket in front, as you saw it just now. I was in the tavern at Hirzau at eleven last night, as I can call the landlord and ten other men to witness. As I was coming over the mountain, it struck twelve in Bonnal, and just then I heard the Bailiff cursing and working, not a stone's throw from the road. I recognized his voice, and wondered what he could be doing there at midnight, so I followed the sound. But I think the worthy Bailiff must have drunk a little more than was necessary, for he took me, poor sinner that I am, for the Devil himself. And when I saw that he was on the point of moving a boundary in our master's forest, I thought to myself I'd give him a fine fright. So I tied his tools and my stick all together, and dragged them over the rocky road behind me, shouting at the top of my lungs: 'Oh! Ah! Uh! Bailiff! You are mine!' And I was not more than a stone's throw from you, when you crept slowly along with your torches to the Bailiff's assistance. But I didn't want to frighten innocent men with my noise, so I turned and ran up the mountain to my basket, and then went home. This morning at six o'clock I went to the Castle and told my master the story. Now, neighbors, how do you think I could get hold of this story and these tools before daylight this morning, if what I am telling you were not true?"

Some of the peasants scratched their heads, and others laughed.

"If such a thing should happen again, neighbors," added the poulterer, "I have a bit of friendly advice to give the watchman, as well as the honorable community at large, — let loose the biggest dog in the village, and you will soon find the Devil!"

CHAPTER XV.

THE FORGIVING GENEROSITY OF A POOR MAN, AND THE PUNISHMENT OF A MALEFACTOR.

THERE was a general murmur on every side when the poulterer had finished speaking. The peasants were vexed at their stupidity, the rich landowners cursed their folly in promising to divide the common, while the poor rejoiced at the triumph of Arner and their reverend pastor. Arner dismissed the people after a few friendly words, and accompanied the clergyman to the parsonage, where he warmly praised the good man for the faithful discharge of his duties, and added a more substantial token of appreciation, in the shape of a deed of gift of a small tithe-field in the village. Theresa, who stood by her husband's side, placed in the pastor's hands a beautiful bouquet of flowers, which his wife discovered the following morning was bound together by a string of pearls.

In obedience to Arner's summons, Hübel-Rudy now presented himself. With outstretched hand, the nobleman said : " Rudy, my grandfather did you a wrong in taking your meadow from you. But he was himself deceived, and you must try to forgive him."

" Ah, Sir," answered the unfortunate man, " I know well enough that it was not his fault, and even in the depths of my poverty I have never borne a grudge against him. How could he help it, when the Bailiff found false witnesses against me? My good old master often afterwards gave me alms and food, God bless him ! And if, Sir, he had only gone about among us, and talked with us as you have done, things would have been very different."

"You must forget that now, Rudy. The meadow is yours again, and I wish you joy with all my heart."

Rudy tried in vain to express his delight and gratitude. but in a moment tears rushed to his eyes, and clasping his hands, he exclaimed : " O gracious Sir, my mother's blessing is upon me! She said to me before she died : ' Rudy, all will go well with you.' Ah, if she could only have lived to see this day ! "

Arner and the pastor were both much affected, and it was after a pause that the former spoke : " I had almost forgotten to say that the Bailiff is bound to pay you arrears and costs."

"May I say a word?" asked the parson. " It is true, Rudy, that he owes you all the arrears, but he is in very straitened circumstances, and I know you are too kind-hearted to bring him to beggary in his old age. Have pity upon his distress, Rudy ! "

" 1 never should think of the arrears for a moment, reverend Sir. And if the Bailiff is poor, — why, Sir, there is hay enough from the meadow to pasture more than three cows, and if I can keep two, I shall have enough and to spare. So I am very willing to allow the Bailiff hay enough for one cow. as long as he lives."

Arner praised Rudy's resolution, but urged him to take time for reflection before acting upon it, and said as the peasant took his leave : " Below in the parsonage stable you will find a cow, which I give you to reconcile you to my dear grandfather, who did you a wrong. I have given orders that a load of hay shall be carried to your house from the Bailiff's barn ; and if you need any wood to repair your house or stable, you may cut it in my forest."

After Rudy's departure, all those assembled at the parson-

age remained silent for a while, and their eyes were filled
with tears. Presently the children of both families begged
permission to go and see Rudy's poor children, and the parents gave their consent. Arner had brought with him in his
carriage a roasted quarter of veal for the destitute family,
and the pastor's wife had made a nourishing soup to go with
it; Arner's servant was sent ahead with this food, while
the whole party followed. When they entered Rudy's door,
the house seemed to contain nothing but ragged, sickly,
half-starved children ; everything denoted extreme poverty.
"And this Rudy," Arner said to the ladies, "is willing to
give up a third part of the hay from his meadow, to the very
man who has kept him in this state of wretchedness for ten
years ! "
"That must never be !" exclaimed Theresa impetuously.
"I cannot bear to think of that man, with all his children,
giving a single penny that belongs to him to that abandoned
wretch ! "
"My dear," said Arner, "would you restrict the course
of that virtue and generosity which God has so exalted
through suffering and want that it has just brought tears to
your eyes? "
"No, that I will not!" she cried. "Let him give away
all his possessions, if he can ; God will never forsake such
a man."
Arner turned to Rudy, and bade him give his children
something to eat. But little Rudy plucked his father by the
sleeve, and whispered : "Father, I want to carry something
to Gertrude."
Arner caught the last word, and inquired what the child
was saying. Rudy told him of the stolen potatoes, of his
mother's death-bed, and of the constant kindness shown
them by the mason and his wife, adding : "Gracious Sir,
this day is a joyful one indeed ; but I cannot enjoy a single

mouthful, unless I may invite these good people to share it."

It would be too long a story to relate how the women praised the mason's wife, how little Rudy ran in great excitement to invite Leonard and Gertrude to supper, how the worthy couple could not be prevailed upon to come, until Arner sent his servant with express injunctions to that effect, when they appeared abashed and with downcast eyes; and how, despite the kindness of Theresa and the pastor's wife, the children were not quite happy until Gertrude's arrival, when they thronged about her with smiles and caresses. Arner and Theresa stood watching this scene a long time, and took leave silently, with tears in their eyes. "Drive slowly for a while," said Arner to the coachman. As they were mounting the hill, they saw the poulterer approaching, and Theresa said to her husband: "This man ought to have something for his pains, since he is really at the bottom of the whole matter."

"Christopher!" cried Arner, "my wife doesn't think it quite fair for you to have played the Devil for nothing," and reached him a couple of thalers.

"Gracious Sir," said the poulterer with a low bow, "I should like to play the Devil every day of my life!"

"Provided," returned Arner, "you could be sure the dogs were kept chained up."

"Very true, Sir!" was the reply, as the carriage drove on.

In pursuance of Arner's decree, the Bailiff was led that evening to the mile-stone, and compelled to restore everything to its former condition. He was accompanied by an excited and disorderly crowd of villagers; the schoolboys fired missiles at him from the walls and trees, as he went by, while the girls stood hand in hand in long rows behind the wayside hedges, and laughed at the strange procession.

Threats and maledictions were showered upon the Bailiff from every house he passed — except one; in Leonard's cottage no living soul was to be seen, and the doors and windows were closed.

To avoid a repetition of this scene on the following day, the strictest orders were issued that none should be allowed to accompany the prisoner to the gallows, except those who first attended the morning service in the church; and sentinels were posted to prevent any strangers from gaining access to the village and joining the procession. Those who should attend the service, and subsequently witness the Bailiff's punishment, were to conduct themselves with order and propriety, on pain of being detained in Bonnal under arrest.

The parson's sermon on the wretchedness of sin and the joy of righteousness went to the hearts of all his congregation; it seemed as if the Bailiff were a mirror in the pastor's hands, from which each one of the multitude saw his own sins reflected. After his discourse was over, the clergyman descended from the pulpit and talked kindly with the prisoner; and on perceiving that Hummel was faint with hunger and exhaustion, he ordered food and drink to be brought from the parsonage. When the Bailiff's strength was somewhat revived, the procession set forth, the pastor walking by his side and praying aloud all the way, while the people followed in deep silence, and the death-bell of Bonnal tolled its solemn knell.

Arrived at the spot, the Bailiff, with bare feet and uncovered head, stood before the multitude, and was made to repeat three times the words: " Here I have deserved to die ! "

A hangman answered in a loud voice: " Yes, thou hast deserved that thy bones should rot here, and the birds of heaven feed upon thy flesh ! "

Three times the Bailiff made answer: " I have deserved it ! "

" Servant of justice, he is pardoned! Kill him not! " cried
the powerful voice of the judge.

" What shall I do to him, then? "

" Thou shalt bind him to the arms of the gallows, and
after fastening his hand to a stake, thou shalt paint the fingers of the perjurer thrice, with an indelible black dye."

During the execution of this sentence, the judge, turning
to the people, pronounced the following injunction:
" Hearken, ye people! Your master and father bids me
say to you that whosoever among you does not dread such a
disgrace more than death, he and his are on the high road to
the same misery in which this poor man is involved! "

CHAPTER XVI.

DOMESTIC ORDER AND DISORDER.

As long as the death-bell tolled in the village, Gertrude prayed at home with her children. She then resolved, in accordance with her promise to the dying Catharine, to pay a visit to her good neighbor Hübel-Rudy, and see what assistance she could render after his change of fortune. She found the children had just risen from their beds, and the father himself looked as if he had not yet had time to dress himself properly. The children's clothes lay scattered about the floor, and the cat was seated on the table, beside the dirty plate from which she had eaten her supper the night before. Gertrude tried to make Rudy comprehend what would be the result if such a condition of things continued, but at first he hardly seemed to understand of what she was speaking. At length he answered, with tears in his eyes: "You are right, neighbor; but, indeed, it could not be otherwise while we were so wretchedly poor."

"That is the very reason, Rudy, why you must be willing to have help and advice now; for this is a deep-rooted disease, which you must set to work in earnest to cure."

"Oh, I suppose the disease will cure itself when I have enough to eat, and am not tormented by the hunger of my children."

"Don't deceive yourself! It will not be so easy as you think to accustom yourself to good, orderly habits. But, Rudy, we will waste no time in talking; we will go to work

at once. Before the sun sets, this room must look so differently that nobody will know it. Tables, windows and floor
must all be scrubbed, and the room must be aired every day.
I am sure your children look so sickly just because they have
no pure air to breathe, day or night. It was a misfortune
that your wife neglected her household so toward the last!
However poor a woman is, she ought at least to do for her
husband and children what costs nothing."

"So my mother often told her; but she was so utterly
broken down by our poverty, that she did not even try to do
what she could. Ever since yesterday it has seemed to me
as if she ought to come back and share my prosperity, as
she did my adversity."

"She is better off than any of us now, Rudy! But the
best way of cherishing her memory is to bring up your children so that they shall not be as unhappy as she. Believe
me, in bringing up a child, trifles are of very great impor-
tance, such as whether it gets up half an hour earlier or
later in the morning, and whether it throws its Sunday
clothes into a corner, or folds them up carefully and lays
them away; and it is very necessary that children should
not be left to themselves all day, but that they should know,
from the time they get up in the morning till they go to bed
at night, just what they have to do. If these little things
are not regarded, the most docile and happy-hearted girl,
when she grows up and has children of her own, may
become so despondent and unlike herself that no one would
recognize her."

"So it was with my wife," sighed Rudy.

"I knew her parents," resumed Gertrude. "There was
never any order in the household; and then she fell into the
hands of the Parson Flieg, who filled her head with dreams
and speculations about the revelation of St. John, as if she
had nothing in the world to do but read about them."

"Yes, I was sometimes afraid she would set the house on fire, she was so absent-minded over her books. They were her sanctuary and her heaven, so that she forgot me and the children and everything else."

"That is a sad state of things!" remarked Gertrude. "Books should be to a woman like her Sunday gown, and work like her everyday clothes."

"She wore this Sunday gown every day."

"Until it was so badly worn as not even to be fit for an everyday dress."

"What made me feel worst of all," said Rudy, "was that with all her slovenliness, she was always so pious, and made the children say their prayers."

"Ah, but there can be no true piety without energy, and when one is slovenly, one can neither pray properly one's self, nor teach it to one's children."

"You are right; when she no longer had her usual food, she began to neglect her books, and instead of praying with the children, only wept over them."

"Let that be a warning to you, Rudy! Teach your children to pray, that they may be willing to work, and to work, that they may never grow tired of praying."

"I will send the two oldest at once to a seamstress, to learn to sew."

"But you must clothe them first, before they can go out of this room."

"Well, then, buy them some cloth for clothes; I know nothing of such things. I will borrow the money to-day."

"Borrow nothing, Rudy. I will buy the cloth, and you shall pay me after the hay harvest."

"Why not borrow?"

"Because it is a part of good house-keeping never to take a thing from one nail to hang it on another, and because out of a hundred men who lend money, there are not ten who do not take an undue advantage. You must learn to keep what God has given back to you and your children after your long suffering.''

Rudy asked Gertrude in some concern whether she then disapproved of his promise to divide the crop of his meadow with the Bailiff. She had not heard of the project, and although it seemed to her hastily conceived, she could not but praise the forgiving generosity which had dictated it. While they were talking, Gertrude washed the children, combed their hair with a gentleness to which they were not accustomed, and made them put on their clothes with more care than usual. Then, bringing a tub, a broom and some brushes from her own house, she set about cleaning the room. After showing Rudy how to continue the work with the aid of the children, she returned home, telling him to send the children to her in the afternoon, if they had been good and helpful. When she had gone, Rudy stood still for a little while, and thought within himself: '' It would be like being in heaven to have such a wife!'' And when he sent the children to her in the afternoon, for the first time in many years he took pains to see that their faces and hands were clean, and their hair and clothes in order, so that they themselves were surprised, and the neighbors who saw them go by said to each other: '' He surely means to marry again!''

The mason's children were all at their spinning-wheels, and although they greeted their guests joyfully, they did not stop working for a moment. '' Hurry and get through, and then you can play with your little friends till six o'clock,'' said Gertrude. Rudy's children stood in open-mouthed wonder at the beautiful work and the cheerful aspect of the room. '' Can you spin?'' she asked.

'' No,'' they answered.

'' Then you must learn, my dears. My children wouldn't

sell their knowledge of it at any price, and are happy enough on Saturday, when they each get their few kreutzers. The year is long, my dears, and if we earn something every week, at the end of the year there is a lot of money, without our knowing how we came by it."

"Oh, please teach us!" implored the children, nestling close to the good woman.

"Willingly," Gertrude replied; "come every day, if you like, and you will soon learn."

Meanwhile, the others had finished their work, and put away their yarn and wheels; they took their visitors by the hand, and all the children sprang merrily about in the meadow under the trees. Gertrude's children were more careful than their companions to avoid the mud and the thorns, and took heed to their clothes. They tied up their stockings and shoes when they became undone, and would often say to Rudy's children: "You are losing your garter," or "You are getting dirty," or "You will tear your dress on the thorns." Their playfellows took it all in good part, for they saw that the mason's children did everything themselves which they prescribed, and were not putting on airs.

On the stroke of six, Gertrude's children ran into the house, like birds to their nests at sundown. "Will you come with us? We are going to pray now," they said to their visitors; and as they were playing the game called "cat's tail," they led the long procession through the meadow, up the steps, and to the very table where they seated themselves. "Must you not go home to prayers, my dears?" inquired Gertrude of the little strangers.

"We don't pray till we go to bed," replied the eldest.

"And when must you go to bed?"

"How do I know?" said the child; and another answered: "When it begins to grow dark."

"Well, then, you can pray with us, and then it will be

time for you to go home." Gertrude heard her own children pray in turn, and then, after letting Rudy's children repeat the prayers they knew, she accompanied them to the corner of the house with a cheery parting, bidding them come again soon.

CHAPTER XVII.

DISTURBANCE REIGNS THROUGHOUT THE VILLAGE, EXCEPT IN
ONE HOUSE.

THROUGH his sympathetic kindness, the pastor so won the
confidence of the imprisoned Bailiff that the latter related to
him in detail the history of his life, involving, as it did, the
life of the whole village, so that the pastor could look into
every household and see the hidden springs of action, clear
as in a mirror. It would be impossible to describe the universal panic which prevailed at the intelligence that the
Bailiff was confessing everything to the pastor. Everywhere people put their heads together mysteriously, and pale,
frightened faces were seen. Husbands and wives who had
been quarrelling suddenly became friends, and the most
obstinate children all at once grew docile and obedient. Circumstances and events which had long been forgotten were
mentioned without any apparent connection, and on every
side the compassion which the Bailiff had excited vanished
as speedily as it had come. The overseers were the most
anxious, and calling a meeting of all the well-to-do peasants
in the village, they resolved to bribe the Bailiff to silence.
All their efforts in this direction, however, were vain, and
they accordingly bent their energies on making mischief
between Arner and the pastor.

About this time, a report began to circulate that everything had not been as it should be at the last assembly of
the people, and that the poulterer had blinded everybody with
devil's tricks. The overseers were the most eager in dis-

seminating this nonsense, since it suited their own schemes. Many an old ghost-story was brought to light under the present state of things. People talked of haunted houses, and recalled the story of the crow which used to come and sit on a particular branch of the smith's tree, whenever a misfortune was in store for him, until he finally cut down the tree, and burned it up; and since then, nothing but good luck had befallen his house, — except, to be sure, that the smith himself had lost his wits, and had to be bound hand and foot. The mothers talked to their children of the black man who would come and catch them if they were naughty, and the wife of the younger Kienholz, who had taught her children to ridicule the idea of ghosts and witches, in order to curry favor with the pastor, now made them recite the prayer against bad spirits every morning and evening.

Even the innocent game of " cat's tail," which Leonard's and Rudy's children played together, was made a cause of suspicion and gossip. The cheesemonger's wife, who seemed to have been born for the express purpose of extracting poison from honey, and making elephants out of gnats, unluckily met Rudy's daughter Maggie in the street, and resolved to get to the bottom of the mysterious game which people were beginning to shake their heads over. She gave her hand to the child with apparent friendliness, and the fol-lowing cross-examination took place:

" Did you children have a good play at the mason's yes-terday? "

" That we did! "

" Was there a pretty cat in the room, my child? "

" Yes."

" A black one? "

" Coal-black."

" But she had fiery eyes? "

" Yes, when she was under the bench."

" What did the cat do? "

" Nothing."

" Did she sit still all the time? "

" No, she came rubbing against our legs, and once almost jumped up in my lap."

" During prayers? "

" Do you suppose cats know when we are praying? "

" Did you touch her? "

" Yes indeed."

" During prayers? "

" Yes, when she came too near us."

" Don't you have to fold your hands while you pray? "

" To be sure."

" Then how could you touch her? "

" With our legs under the table."

" But she was coal-black, wasn't she? "

" Not all over."

" But almost black? "

" Yes."

" And she had fiery eyes? "

" I told you so, when she was under the bench."

From this conversation, which was immediately reported right and left, with numerous additions, the rumor soon spread that the cat in question was no ordinary cat, and that things were not as they should be in the mason's household. For a long time no one said anything of the matter to Leonard or Rudy, but they noticed that people looked at them strangely, and the children often came home in tears, complaining that the nicest children in the village refused to play with them. Finally a neighbor came to the mason, and told him that one of the chief gossips of the place, who went by the name of " Glib-tongued Peg," had been circulating wonderful stories about his family, and mentioned the absurd rumors which were going the rounds. Leonard turned pale

with anger, and no longer master of himself, ran like a mad-
man to Peg's house. She was outside at the well, with some
of her cronies, to whom she had just been relating the story
afresh, and was so alarmed by his sudden appearance and
the angry accusations with which he assailed her, that she
immediately took back her words, and confessed in the presence of all the by-standers that her slanders had no foundation.

This put an end to the persecution of the mason's household, but the peasants were all the more zealous in decrying
the poulterer, and in asserting that he had hoodwinked them
all by his magic arts. When Christopher came to Bonnal, as
usual, to buy chickens, pigeons and eggs for the Castle, no
one would sell him so much as an egg-shell, and he was not
allowed to enter a single house. At a loss what to do,
the poulterer finally seated himself with his basket on the
bench beside the dwelling of his old friend Leupi, exclaiming in vexation: " My Devil's job and the fee I got for it
have turned out badly for me, neighbor ! "

" God forbid that you should engage in such a thing for
the sake of a fee ! " cried Leupi, rising from the bench, and
withdrawing from so dangerous a neighborhood.

An hour later, the whole village was in possession of the
intelligence that the poulterer had himself confessed to
having a compact with the Devil. This rumor was an addi-
tional encouragement to the rich peasants and overseers, in
their resolution to prevent the promised division of the common. The only question was, how this end was to be accomplished. They would have preferred to withdraw their consent
openly, on the ground that the promise had been extorted
from them on false pretences, but as their courage was not
sufficient for this, they took council together as to the best
means of putting off the evil day. Two opinions prevailed ;
one was, to postpone the matter until the autumn, and then

represent to Arner the impossibility of dividing the meadow
at that season, when they were all over-crowded with cattle,
and not in condition to dispense with the common pasture-
ground. The other recommendation was to give up a certain
piece of the land to be divided by way of trial, selecting for
the purpose a worthless corner of the meadow, full of thorns
and swamps, which it would be impossible to cultivate properly, so that Arner would be indignant at the apparent
laziness of those to whom it was intrusted. After a long
discussion, it was decided to adopt both of these counsels,
and to bring them before Arner by means of the new Bailiff
Meyer. The latter objected at first to being employed as a
tool in such an enterprise, but his scruples were overcome
by the persuasions and ridicule of his influential fellow-
townsmen.

Meanwhile, no one suspected that Arner was employing a
portion of almost every day in becoming acquainted with
the common in question, examining thoroughly the whole
conformation of the land, and deciding just which portions
were good for pasturage, which for agriculture, and which
were only fit for reeds and lumber.

The only cottage in the village which was free from the
turbulent unrest of this period was that of Gertrude. She
alone seemed to possess a soul untainted by the moral filth
around her, and always had a stock of mottoes on hand
which made the path of duty plainer for herself and others.
Some of these were : " Be silent about everything which
does not concern you" ; " Do not speak of that which you
do not understand" ; " Step aside when people speak either
too loud or too softly" ; " Learn well what it is necessary
for you to use" ; " Let your head and heart always be in the
right place, and never in many at once, but always with
you" ; " Serve with body and soul those to whom you are
indebted, and those you love." Guided by such sayings as

these, she had attained to a remarkable degree of domestic and social wisdom, and throughout the confusion which reigned in the village, no word escaped her lips which could give rise to misunderstandings, not a syllable which could provoke either enmity or ridicule.

Rudy's children came to her almost every day, and constantly learned from her to take more heed to themselves and all about them. While they were spinning and sewing, she taught them to count and cipher, for she regarded arithmetic as the foundation of all intellectual order. Her method was to let the children count their threads or stitches both forwards and backwards, and add and subtract, multiply and divide the result by different numbers. The children vied with each other in this game, trying to see who could be quickest and surest in the exercise. When they were tired, they sang songs, and night and morning Gertrude prayed with them. Her favorite prayer, and the one she taught the children first, was as follows:

O God so good and kind,
Of all our gifts the spring,
Without whom nothing is,
From whom comes everything, —
A healthy body give,
And grant that in this frame
The soul unharmed may live,
The conscience pure remain.

CHAPTER XVIII.

IT IS ONLY FRIENDS IN NEED THAT ARE FRIENDS INDEED.

THE exhortations of the good pastor had awakened such a
sense of hopeless remorse in the Bailiff, that he felt as if no
one in the world could look upon him with compassion. He
often sat motionless in the parson's room, his eyes filled with
tears, and sometimes refused to drink the wine which was
placed before him. One day, while he was in this state, the
door opened, and Hübel-Rudy entered. The Bailiff gazed
at him a few moments speechless with terror, then sinking
on his knees, he implored forgiveness of the injured man.
"Rise, Bailiff!" said the pastor; "he has long since forgiven you."

They helped the wretched man to his feet, and he confessed, trembling, that it had seemed to him as if Rudy's
mother would certainly appear behind her son. "But you
know she is dead," said Rudy.

"I know it! Yet it seemed as if she must be here to
reproach me for her wrongs. I suppose she cursed me with
her dying breath for all I made her suffer."

"No, Bailiff, God be praised!" exclaimed the pastor;
"the good Catharine forgave and prayed for you in her last
hours, and wished you all manner of good."

Rudy repeated the dying message of his mother, which
brought sweetest comfort to the soul of the repentant man.
When the pastor told him of Rudy's generous offer to allow
him fodder for one cow from his newly recovered meadow,

Hummel was too much moved to speak ; yet for the first time since his captivity he felt strengthened and refreshed.

The Bailiff's wife, meanwhile, was in a wretched condition. Prostrated by the fright and sorrow of the last few days, she had unfortunately fallen into the hands of the quack doctor Treufaug, who gave her some of his so-called " heavenly drops," which rapidly increased her bad symptoms without her suspecting the cause. When the Bailiff heard of her illness, he obtained permission from the pastor to return home for the night. He found his wife much changed in his absence, but she rejoiced to see him, and the two talked long and confidentially together of all that had befallen them since their separation.

" Do you know," she asked presently, " who has shown me most kindness during this time? But you would never guess. Hans Wüst has come every evening since you were taken prisoner, and has split wood, drawn water, and done whatever I needed. Then Hübel-Rudy and Gertrude have been very kind ; but she is angry now because I would take Treufaug's medicine, which she says she knows has poisoned a great many people."

" I certainly should not have let you take it if I had been here," replied her husband. " But how was it with my friends? I suppose they treated you worst of all?"

" You are pretty nearly right. At first they were very friendly, and made me all sorts of promises, provided I would prevent you from implicating any of them in your statements. But all of a sudden, for no apparent reason, they grew furious against us, and uttered the most dreadful threats. Then Glib-tongued Peg came running to me almost beside herself with rage, after the scene with Leonard at the well, and cried at the top of her voice, so that she could be heard through the whole street : ' It is all your fault ! Yours is a cursed house, and whoever has anything to do with you

gets into trouble!' But Kriecher was worst of all. He has
never lost an opportunity of mocking us in our misfortune,
and the other day he actually thrust out his tongue at me in
the public street, and said we might now be glad ourselves
of the pastor's alms, of which we had tried to defraud him."

"But I'll venture to say he has not done that since last
Wednesday," said the Bailiff.

"You are right; but why?"

"Because he had his reward Tuesday night. You know
every Tuesday afternoon the beggars come to the parsonage
for bread. Kriecher sent one of his children, with the message that he lay sick in bed and had not a mouthful to eat in
the house. But the pastor was not to be imposed upon, and
sent back word he must come himself, which he finally did
at twilight. I was in the next room, and I never shall forget
the rage with which the pastor brought his fist down on the
table, and took the fellow to task for his meanness. Kriecher
mumbled something about being an unlucky man who was
always slandered, but the pastor bade him depart out of his
sight, and thank Heaven that an aged parson could not use
his cane against him as he deserved."

While the Bailiff and his wife were thus chatting together,
a conspiracy was on foot among the unscrupulous men of the
village, and as the prisoner was returning to his captivity at
five o'clock in the morning, he was suddenly accosted by a
man who lay half concealed behind an old nut-tree near the
path. He started back at first, but his interlocutor, coming close to him, shouted out: "Is it really you, Bailiff?
I thought you were locked up, and here you are in the
street!"

Hummel was convinced by the insolence of the fellow's
manner, and the smell of brandy about him, that he was
the tool of others. All the way to the parsonage the prisoner was pursued by a loud stream of invective, which made

many people rise from their beds and run to the window to inquire the cause of the disturbance. This was precisely what the originators of the plot desired, since if it could become village talk that the Bailiff was allowed to go home at night, this might be reported to Arner, to the prejudice of the pastor. The latter, however, wrote of the affair himself to Arner, as he was just then sending a letter to him by Michael, in the bearer's behalf.

When, after some delay, Michael was admitted to the nobleman's presence, Arner measured him from head to foot with a serious glance, and then bade him give a full account of the robberies which had taken place at the Castle in his grandfather's time. Michael obeyed, and related how he, together with the Bailiff's servants, had taken unthreshed grain from the barns of the Castle, letting it down with ropes into the moat, and conveying it thence to the tavern ; how a hundred times by night he had removed the Castle mark from the best oak and fir trees, and then helped the peasants to cut them down as their own property ; how they had often played at the tavern with the Castle servants for tools, ropes or baskets ; how at the present day many peasants were wearing clothes lined with stolen sacks, while in all the houses round about were portions of wagons and ploughs, wine-casks, etc., bearing the Castle brand, or from which this had been cut ; and how all the trades-people, smith, locksmith, wagoner, carpenter, joiner, tailor and shoemaker, had worked for the Bailiff without wages, in consideration of the various articles he could procure for them from the Castle.

Michael's open, ingenuous manner, and the frankness with which he related the evil practices in which he himself had borne a part, so won Arner's confidence that he conversed with him at some length about the affairs of the village, and dismissed him finally with orders to make out a list of all the goods that had been stolen from the Castle.

CHAPTER XIX.

THE NEW BAILIFF FINDS HIS OFFICE A PERPLEXING ONE.

MICHAEL had scarcely departed before the Bailiff Meyer appeared. He returned Arner's friendly greeting with so constrained a manner, that the nobleman said to himself with a sigh : " He has hardly been Bailiff a week, and looks already as if he could betray his country ! "

Meyer soon began to insinuate that there would be many difficulties in the way of dividing the common, and that in his humble opinion it would be better to make trial first of a small portion of it, for instance, the corner next the forest.

" Which corner do you mean ? " inquired Arner.

" The uppermost corner, between the fir-trees and the hill."

" That one ? " — with a penetrating look.

" Yes, — unless your Grace would prefer another."

" But " (with another sharp glance) " you are speaking of this one ? "

" Yes."

" And you are quite in earnest ? "

" There are many men in the village who hold this opinion."

" And you agree with them ? "

" Yes."

" Are you acquainted with this corner ? "

" Partially."

" You ought to know it thoroughly, since you own some land adjoining."

" I do know it pretty well, gracious Sir."

" But you suppose I do not?"

" I didn't think of that."

" Of what?"

" Of your not knowing it."

" Would you have recommended it to me if you ha supposed I was acquainted with it?"

" I am very sorry."

" For what?"

" For having recommended it to you."

" And why?"

" Because you seem to think it is good for nothing."

" Don't you think so too?"

" I — can't exactly praise it."

" Why, then, did you recommend it to me?"

" The overseers were all agreed that I must do it."

" And what was their object?"

" I do not know."

" That I may believe or not; but at all events, one thing is settled, — not only the corner, but the whole common, must be divided, and that without delay."

" Your Grace will not be angry if I say one word more?" began Meyer anew.

" Certainly not."

" It will hardly be possible to divide the meadow this summer."

" Why not?"

" Because nobody in the village is in condition to keep the cattle in the stalls, and do without the pasturage."

" Is fodder scarce in your village?"

" Yes, they say there is very little, and a great many cattle."

" What do you mean by ' they say '? Don't you know certainly?"

" Not so altogether certainly, gracious Sir."

" Ah, indeed! But you probably know how much fodder you have yourself?"

" Well, yes."

" Have you enough to be able to keep your cattle in the stable?"

" I can't deny that I have."

" And the harvests have been so good this last year that I should suppose all the peasants would be as well off as you. But in order to be sure, it will be well to count the cattle and measure the hay. You must take the beadle with you to-day and do this; then we shall see how far the common is needed this summer."

The terrified Meyer still had one more promise on his conscience, and plucking up courage, stammered that the pastor had been letting the Bailiff out of prison at night.

" Do you report this of your own accord, or at the instigation of others?" asked Arner.

After some hesitation the answer came: " They bade me report it."

" Who?"

" The overseers."

" Their names?"

Deadly pale, Meyer gave the desired information.

" And how," pursued Arner, " did you communicate with these gentlemen? Did you see them separately, or were they all together, when they gave you their commands?"

" They were all together."

" Where?"

" At Kienholz's house."

" And for what purpose?"

" I — don't exactly know. I was only there a moment."

" But I suppose you know what they were doing during that moment?"

"Well, yes, — they were trying to prevent the division of the common."

"And you allowed yourself to be used as a tool, and came to me with lies, to bring about this end?"

The Bailiff stood in guilty silence, with downcast eyes. Arner pitied him, and said: "Meyer, as this is your first offence, I will overlook it; but beware of deceiving me again! Now go, and with the beadle's assistance, do what I bade you. Bring me the list to-morrow."

It was in no enviable frame of mind that the Bailiff returned to the conclave to announce the result of his mediation. His reception was not such as to make him desire to prolong his stay, so he set forth almost immediately in pursuit of the beadle, without suspecting that a messenger from the indignant landowners had preceded him. He was much surprised, as well as vexed, to learn from the beadle's little daughter that her father had just started for market, and would not return before night. He was at first suspicious, and questioned her sharply, but the little maid held stoutly to her assertion, and not until the baffled magistrate had turned his back in disgust, did she burst into a peal of merry laughter at the face of the new Bailiff, who had looked as if he were ready to cry, simply because she had not been able to find her father behind the stove!

The discomfited Meyer returned to Kienholz's house, and told the overseers that one of them must help him in the beadle's place. No one, however, would consent to perform this office, and the Bailiff was fairly nonplussed. At length Hügi suggested that he should let each proprietor make a statement of the amount of hay and the number of cattle he possessed. The Bailiff reflected a moment, and then said: "Well, only the statement must be made on oath."

"Yes, on oath, of course!" answered the peasants, winking at each other. And thus the required list was finally completed.

Early in the morning Meyer carried it to Arner, explain-
ing that it had been impossible to execute his commands to
the letter, owing to the absence of the beadle.

"Why did you not take one of the overseers in his
place?" inquired Arner.

"No one was willing to come."

"Did you tell them it was a matter of moment to me,
and would no one then consent to aid you?"

"No, Sir; all that I could say was in vain."

"Then carry this list back, and read every man's statement to him aloud, in the presence of two of the overseers;
let these sign as witnesses, and then bring the document
back to me, before the village meeting begins."

The peasants were not at all pleased with the idea of rati-
fying their statements in the presence of witnesses; but
they yielded to necessity, and returned the document witnessed in due form. When Arner received it, he bade
Meyer take the beadle, and with Michael and the poulterer
as assistants, go immediately from house to house, and
make out a fresh list, measuring the hay and counting the
cattle with care and precision. He caused the bells to be
rung to assemble the meeting, "for," he said, "I would
rather the proprietors should not be at home during the
counting and measuring; and should any of the wives or
servants oppose your entrance, let Flink arrest them, and
bring them here." Arner then placed a guard at all the
entrances to the square, and ordered the watchmen on no
pretext to allow any one to depart until the meeting was
over.

CHAPTER XX.

A CURIOUS ASSEMBLY.

THE community had soon assembled near the linden-tree; but never in the annals of Bonnal had the peasants conducted themselves so strangely. Many who had always stepped proudly crept along like old crones, hanging their heads; former enemies stood side by side, and whispered confidentially together; people whose tongues had been wont to wag from sunrise to sunset were silent as the grave; men who had always donned their Sunday clothes before going to the village meeting appeared now in working trousers and overalls. Most of them sat there as if at a loss what to say, and many a man asked his neighbor two or three times if he did not think it would rain before night. But some of the overseers, who noticed the universal panic, put a bold face on the matter, and began to talk as if to show they were not afraid. Finally old Trümpi, who had never in his life been known to arrive anywhere in season, appeared with the intelligence that the Bailiff and the beadle were walking down toward the village, in company with Michael and the poulterer, and were carrying with them paper, ink and pens.

This news spread like wildfire through all the benches, carrying consternation with it. It was but a few moments before one man discovered he had forgotten his handkerchief, a second, that his tobacco had been left behind, while a third found it imperatively necessary to speak with his wife a minute, and a fourth remembered he had left something out which might be stolen; one even had the nose-bleed, — in short, a large number of peasants started at once on the homeward road. But the watchman ordered them back, counselling them to borrow tobacco and handkerchiefs from their neighbors, and to stanch the nose-bleed this time at the fountain under the linden-tree.

They accordingly returned to the benches, and the next moment their anxiety was increased by the command that the overseers and landed proprietors, seventeen in number, should go immediately to Arner at the parsonage. In some trepidation they obeyed the summons, but it was in vain that the nobleman tried to induce them to a voluntary confession. He had hardly done speaking when Kalberleder burst out: "We understand neither your words nor your accusation!"

"Who are the 'we' in whose name you speak?" returned Arner.

"Oh, nobody, — I speak only in my own name."

"No, Kalberleder, you have come to an agreement beforehand, and that is why the 'we' slipped out. But you ask what my charge is? Then hear it: you have embezzled the public property, tampered with the public accounts, and shown yourselves faithless and perjured with respect to everything which came into your hands!"

This was certainly explicit, and much worse than they had expected. They looked at each other a while in silence. Then one of them plucked up courage to demand a judicial investigation, and the others followed his lead, protesting their innocence.

"It is enough!" said Arner. "From this moment you are prisoners. You will now return with a guard to your places in the meeting, but are forbidden to exchange a word with any one. Away!"

A deadly silence fell upon the assembly as the seventeen men entered under guard. Arner followed, and bade the rest of the people be seated, while the culprits stood before him.

He then ordered the clerk to read aloud the list of articles which had been stolen from the Castle by the prisoners. He read : " In the stable of Judge Kienast are two wheels which were stolen from the Castle ; Kalberleder's wheel-barrow was stolen from the Castle," etc. Sixteen of the seventeen men were implicated in the charges, and they stood there, terrified and confused, not heeding Arner's admonition, joined to the exhortations of their friends, that they should confess their guilt. But the honest old Renold, who had long watched the evil practices of his colleagues with a heavy heart, stood forth pale and trembling, and thus spoke : " Sire, I am an old gray-headed man, and God knows that I have never had any pleasure in the wickedness prevailing among us ; but your charges are quite true."

" Old man," Arner replied ; " your gray hairs fill me with compassion. I well know that you have only erred in keeping silence regarding the evil practices of the rest, and it grieves me that you have been associated with people who refuse to acknowledge their manifest guilt." He turned angrily to the others as he spoke, but their spirit was at last broken, and sinking on their knees, they begged for mercy.

At this moment, the men who had been sent to the village to measure the hay and count the cattle, appeared with their new list. Arner compared it carefully with the previous one, and found that twenty-two peasants had made false statements regarding their possessions, including the whole sixteen who were on their knees before him. He caused the other six to be summoned from their places, and four at once presented themselves. The sacrist and the school-master, however, lingered. They were no landed pro-prietors, properly speaking, but had made fraudulent state-ments about their trifling belongings, aping the wealthy peasants out of sheer pride.

" Are these two not here ? " inquired Arner.

"Indeed they are!" cried out some of the men from the furthermost benches.

"Who says we are not?" said the sacrist, advancing to the front with the schoolmaster, and making a reverence in due form. Then with folded hands and sanctimoniously upturned eyes, he began: "Ah, gracious Sir, I have not a handful of fodder except what comes from the poor little churchyard; and I had the misfortune to miscalculate in regard to the petty bit of hay."

"What was the amount of your mistake?" asked Arner, after eying him searchingly for a few moments.

"One cord."

"And how much fodder did you get from your churchyard?"

"They say now it is two cords."

"Indeed? But I suppose what they say is true?"

"Well — yes."

"And how much did you state you had?"

"One cord."

"Of all the rascals here, I doubt if there is one who has made a mistake of half the whole amount, as you have done!"

The sacrist being silenced, the schoolmaster now begged permission to say a word, and proceeded to declare that one of his two cows had been taken from his barn a few days ago, without his knowledge. "I am very sorry," he added, "but I quite forgot that the butcher of Rebstal had come after her."

"You must suffer from a poor memory," remarked Arner.

"Yes, Sir, for some time past; and then my wife takes more care of the barn; I am busy with the school."

"Then you ought to have let your wife make the statement about the number of the cattle; or you ought to have gone into the barn to see whether you had two cows or one."

The cattle-dealer Stoffel here arose and said : " But, indeed, gracious Sir, I am quite innocent, for I am expecting the cattle every day which I mentioned."

" Nobody asked you how many you were expecting, but how many you had," returned Arner.

" That is true, Sir ; but as I was expecting the cattle every hour, I had to take account of them for the pasturage."

" You said there were eight more than you really have, did you not? "

" Your Grace is right."

" From whom did you purchase them? "

" They are coming from different places."

" When do you expect them? "

" In three days at latest."

" All eight? "

" Quite certainly."

" Your plea is in order, if it is true."

Here four others arose with a similar story, and finally the schoolmaster hopped up, declaring that he was also expecting a cow, for he had only exchanged his for another. Then Arner said : " Neighbors, you must not forget that you were all convicted of dishonesty and deceit, even before your cattle or your hay were thought of ; and you will find it quite natural that I should take measures to convince myself that you are speaking the truth. You will remain here in the Castle three days, until your cattle arrive."

An awful silence ensued. " What is the matter? " inquired Arner.

For a moment there was no reply, and then Stoffel faltered : " My — my purchases are not yet quite in order."

" Did you not just say that all eight of your cattle would certainly come by the day after to-morrow? "

" Yes, if I can go home, I am sure they will."

" But if you stay, seven will surely come? "

No answer.

" Look here, if only six come, I will be satisfied."

Again there was no reply.

" Well, surely three or four will come, at least?"

" All eight, if I can send word."

" What sort of word?"

" That they shall be sent to me."

" And without this message not a single one will come?"

" No, I don't suppose there will."

" Neither do I, nor have I thought so at all, any more than I believe that the schoolmaster has exchanged his cow with the butcher."   And Arner proceeded to talk seriously to all those present about the evils of deceit and lying.

CHAPTER XXI.

ARNER METES OUT JUSTICE, AND A DYING WOMAN ASKS
FORGIVENESS.

ATTRACTED by a sound of loud talking from the benches,
Arner perceived that the peasants were beginning to express
their condemnation of the poor malefactors kneeling before
him. "I wish I could believe," he said, "that those of you
who are sitting on the benches were better than these men in
front; but I know only too well that there is hardly a house
in the village which does not contain many articles belonging
to the Castle, and that some of you are even sitting here
before me in coats that are lined with grain-bags from my
store-house."

The words had hardly left his lips before Hartknopf laid
his coat tightly together over his knees, and grew red as
fire. His conduct was so remarkable that it drew the attention of his neighbors, who turned over the lappets of his
coat to inspect the lining. Such a burst of laughter arose
that Arner inquired the cause.

"Hartknopf has the Castle mark on his coat-lining!"
shouted one man.

"I bought this lining ten years ago!" cried Hartknopf in
a rage.

"But this is the brand of the new sacks, which are under
five years old!" exclaimed another.

"If I were you," said Arner, "I would restore quiet to
the assembly by carrying my coat home." And with this
suggestion the old hypocrite was forced to comply.

Arner commanded the beadle to seat twelve of the poorest old men in the parish in the places of the overseers, and compelled the twenty-two to kneel down before them and publicly beg for pardon. The clerk read aloud the false and correct statement of each man regarding his cattle and hay, and he was obliged to acknowledge the truth in the presence of the whole community. Arner then dismissed the assembly until afternoon.

At the second session he brought up his project about the division of the common, showing the peasants that by employing the abundant springs he had discovered to irrigate their land, a large part of the pasture-ground might be converted into excellent meadow-land, so that each member of the community could derive an income of three or four hundred florins from his portion. Just as the inhabitants of Bonnal were beginning to exchange their fear of their master for something approaching confidence, the poulterer of Arnheim appeared, with complaints regarding his recent treatment in the village. Arner noticed that many of the peasants looked ashamed, and some of them said aloud: "The poulterer's sorceries will soon be forgotten, since the meadow is divided!"

Without heeding these remarks, the nobleman said gravely: "Every one of you may believe what he pleases, but I must prevent you from wronging others in consequence of your belief. If any man has a complaint against the poulterer, let him come forward and state it, and I will see that justice is done." But no one spoke. Arner went on: "Your silence does not satisfy me. I could have thought some of the accused here before me might feel moved to confess that this treatment of the poulterer was all a plot to prevent the division of the common."

The overseers looked at each other, and Renold besought them to make the required confession. For the first time in

their lives, they followed his advice ; and thus the affair with
the poulterer was finally ended

While they were still sitting beneath the linden-tree, the
pastor's servant came to say that the Bailiff's wife was convinced she had been poisoned by Treufaug's medicines, and
petitioned that her husband might be allowed to come to her
before she died. The benevolent look faded from Arner's
face, and in a terrible voice, which had never been heard
from him before, he commanded the beadle to go to the house
of the so-called physician, and bring him hither without delay. The beadle, who was no friend to the quack doctor,
soon returned with the intelligence that Treufaug, standing
at the window in his wig, had sent word that he was lying
sick in bed and could not come. "Well, then," said Arner
with a bitter laugh, "bring the man to me on a litter, that
the journey may not harm him." Dozens of the younger
men sprang at once to do his bidding.

Now after the beadle's departure, Treufaug's mind was
ill at ease, and taking his old spy-glass from the wall, he
levelled it upon the public square below. He could see the
sarcastic expression of Arner's face, and it made him trem-
ble. Presently he observed that the nobleman was surrounded by a number of people with litters, and felt reässured, thinking that something else must be on foot. He
had just returned from the cellar with a bottle of wine, with
which he proposed to revive himself after his fright, when he
heard a loud knocking at the door, and looking from the
window, beheld a litter surrounded by a large crowd. All
resistance and protestations were in vain ; he was obliged to
place himself upon the mattress, and allow himself to be
covered with the upper feather-bed, and thus was carried in
triumph through the village.

When the litter was set down under the linden-tree, and
the indignant physician, springing from the bed, began to

protest against the treatment he had received, an uncontrollable laughter broke out among the people, and even Arner himself could hardly command a sober face. Presently, however, the nobleman restrained his mirth, and said seriously: "I have previously forbidden you to use your hangman's drops; but I now revoke that command. Use them on as many people as are willing to be killed by you; but if anybody dies on your hands, you must make his grave. And since you are old and short of breath, so that you can hardly bear the labor of digging, you can lend some day-laborer your gray coat with the many buttons, and your black wig; then you shall sit by and look on, while he digs the grave in your stead." With this sentence he dismissed the offender, and the meeting soon after came to an end.

The good pastor hastened to the Bailiff's dying wife, and sat awhile silent beside her, attentive to her every want, and with a face full of tender compassion. Presently she seemed to suffer less pain, and he ventured to express a wish already hovering on her lips, that she would see all the poor people whom she and her husband had wronged, and ask their forgiveness before her death. From her bedside the good man went to see Treufaug, and partly by the threat of a *post mortem* examination, but still more by kindly persuasion and exhortation, he induced the misguided doctor to admit that he had no sure knowledge of the power and effect of his drugs, and obtained from him the promise that he would never use them again on his own responsibility.

Early the next morning, the poor people assembled at the door of the dying woman. She was already awake, and it was Gertrude's gentle hand which smoothed her pillow and wiped the sweat from her brow. The pastor went out and told the assembled men, women and children, nearly forty in number, to come in as quietly as possible. Most of them drew off their heavy wooden shoes, and entering the sick-room on tiptoe, they all answered the silent greeting of their hostess with a friendly nod, and sat down noiselessly on the chairs and benches which Gertrude had arranged for them. The Bailiff's wife addressed her visitors, thanking them for complying with her request, and begging their forgiveness for all the evil they had suffered at her hands. She closed with a petition that all would utter a prayer for the welfare of her soul, and sank back unconscious on her pillow. The pastor fell on his knees and prayed silently, while the eyes of all present were filled with tears of pity and forgiveness. Then at a sign from the clergyman, they silently withdrew from the chamber of death.

CHAPTER XXII.

PLANS OF REGENERATION IN BONNAL.

As the Sunday approached when Arner had decreed that
Hummel should be exposed to the view of the whole congregation, while the pastor held up his previous life as a warning to those present, the prisoner expressed the utmost horror
of this penalty, declaring that he would rather have his punishment at the gallows repeated, than stand under the pulpit
to be the laughing-stock of the town. He represented that
such a ceremony could neither dispose him to thoughts of
repentance, nor have a beneficial effect upon the spectators.
The pastor was finally so moved by his entreaties, as well as
convinced of the reasonableness of his plea, that he inter-
ceded with Arner, and induced him to remit the sentence.[1]
Accordingly, the clergyman merely took Hummel's life as a
text, preaching a stirring sermon against the wickedness and
corruption which had been fostered so long in their midst,
and which were still rife, in almost equal measure, in the
hearts of many of his listeners.

This discourse everywhere made a profound impression ;
the peasants could talk of nothing else on the way home, and
Arner, pressing the good pastor's hand, thanked him heartily
for his edifying words. He expressed, at the same time, an
earnest desire to labor for the improvement of the village,

---

[1] In the earlier editions of this work, the original plan of the
Bailiff's punishment was adhered to. It is a sign of advancing civili-
zation that in the edition of 1819 Arner's sentence was revoked as
above.

and asked the clergyman if he could recommend an upright, able man from among the people, who could help him in furthering his designs. The parson mentioned at once the spinner known as Cotton Meyer, and proposed they should visit him and his sister that afternoon. They were accompanied by the Lieutenant Glülphi, one of Arner's aids in regulating the economic conditions of his government.

Cotton Meyer was sitting at his door with a child in his lap, when the three gentlemen approached, and had no suspicion that they were seeking him, until they paused before his garden gate. Then he went to meet them with so calm and dignified a bearing that Glülphi did not give him his hand, as he usually did to the peasants, and Arner addressed him less familiarly than was his wont when speaking to his dependants.

The visitors were about to seat themselves on the bench under the apple-tree; but Meyer led them into the parlor, where his sister was sitting by the table, nodding over the open Bible, as was her custom on Sunday afternoons. She started up with a cry as the door opened, and straightening her cap, closed the Bible; then, taking a sponge, she moistened it in a tin hand-basin which shone like silver, and erased the chalk figures with which her brother had covered the table, despite the remonstrance of the strangers, who feared that Meyer might have further use for his reckoning. After wiping the table carefully, she brought a large fine linen table-cloth, and laid new tin plates, with knives, forks and heavy silver spoons upon it.

" What are you doing? " inquired her guests; " we have already dined."

" I suppose so," answered Maria; " but since you have come into a peasant's house, you must take kindly to our peasant ways." Running into the kitchen, she returned with two plates of little cakes and a fine large ham, and Arner,

Glülphi and the pastor seated themselves good-naturedly
before the shining dishes.

When the visitors began to praise the house, the garden
and the whole establishment, Maria remarked that twenty
years ago they had been among the poorest in the village.
" I know it," said Arner, " and I wonder at your prosperity
the more, as the weavers and spinners have usually turned
out the most good-for-nothing people in the country."

Meyer was forced to admit that this was true, but denied
that the cause lay in the industry itself. The trouble was,
he said, that these poor people were not in the habit of laying
up anything from their earnings, and led wretched, aimless
lives. He felt sure that Arner might find many ways of
winning the hearts of the people, so as to lead them into
better paths, and suggested, as one expedient, that he should
promise to every child, which up to its twentieth year should
annually lay aside ten florins from its earnings, a field free
from tithes. " But," went on Meyer, " after all, we can do
very little with the people, unless the next generation is to
have a very different training from that our schools furnish.
The school ought really to stand in the closest connection
with the life of the home, instead of, as now, in strong con-
tradiction to it."

Glülphi joined in the conversation with eagerness, and
argued that a true school should develop to the fullest extent
all the faculties of the child's nature. The question next
arose, how such a school could be established in Bonnal.
Cotton Meyer, when appealed to, rejoined: " I know a
spinning-woman in the village who understands it far better
than I"; and he went on to tell the others such things of
Gertrude's little school and its effects upon her children, that
they resolved to visit her and examine her method for themselves. They also spoke of the corruption prevailing in the
village, and discussed the best method of choosing a good

bailiff. Cotton Meyer showed himself through it all a man of such clear judgment and practical common sense, that his guests left him with a feeling of respect almost approaching veneration.

CHAPTER XXIII.

MUCH APPREHENSION AND ONE PEACEFUL HOME.

AFTER the morning service, Arner had given orders to the
beadle to announce in the village that on the following
Thursday the common would be divided, and on Friday
every one who was in Hummel's debt must settle accounts
with him under the linden-tree. All Bonnal was panic-
stricken at this news, and the good impression made by the
sermon vanished as quickly as it had come. As Cotton
Meyer's sister walked along the street, she saw groups of
frightened-looking spinning-girls putting their heads together,
and when she addressed them, the greater number cast down
their eyes and made no answer. After a while, one or two
ventured to stammer that they owed money to Hummel, and
must go under the linden on Friday; then, gaining courage,
many of them seized her hands, imploring her to intercede
for them with their parents, who knew nothing of their
debts.

But it was by no means the children alone who looked
forward with apprehension to the day of reckoning; the
parents were in many cases in a similar situation. One
woman had pawned a garment which her husband missed
from the wash; another had carried a cloak to Hummel, and
then asserted that a beggar had stolen it. Most pathetic of
all was the despair ot the so-called "Pious Barbara," who
was so overcome with the shame in store for her, that she
privately resolved to send a poor woman of the same name
in her place on Friday.

Gertrude's house was again almost the only one in the village which was undisturbed by dark forebodings. The parents spoke together with joyful emotion of the morning's sermon, and Gertrude read several chapters aloud from the Bible, beside singing a hymn with the children. After the afternoon service, the whole family gathered about the hearth, for it had grown chilly. As they sat there, Gertrude said with tears in her eyes: " Our single aim, after all, is that we may be all together in eternity as we are now."

Leonard rejoined: " Our being so together on earth, as we now are, will surely lead to our being together in heaven."

And little Harry cried: " Yes, how beautiful it is to sit so around the hearth! Say, mother, don't people grow good, when they sit together so, and talk of God, and pray and sing?" The domestic hearth was sacred to the ancients, but it is doubtful whether any one has ever made a better eulogy upon it than our little friend Harry.

It seemed, in truth, as if that humble fireside grew daily more blessed. Everybody had thought that, as soon as Leonard found it possible to earn money, he would fall back into his old ways. But it was not so. He rose early, cleaned out the stall, milked the cow, and did many things he had previously left to his wife, and went off merrily to his work, with the children's morning hymn ringing in his ears. When he reached the churchyard, to be sure, his cheerful mood would usually vanish, for although the apprentices were tolerably faithful, most of the day-laborers were lazy and good-for-nothing, and made their master much trouble.

Still, his home joys compensated for all the annoyances which befell him. In the evening he helped his oldest son to build a Tower of Babel, such as was pictured in his grandmother's Bible, out of a heap of clay ; and taught him to calculate the amount of lime and stone and sand necessary

to construct a given length of wall. One day he bought
Nicholas a mason's hod and apron, and no prince was ever
prouder at the first wearing of his crown, than the mason's
boy, when he donned the implements of his future calling.

Usually, when Leonard came home, he found Rudy's children in the house. They came every day to learn to spin,
and the love and patience with which Gertrude bore with
these disorderly and untrained little ones, was almost past
belief. Their eyes were often anywhere but on their yarn,
so that this would now be too thick, and now too thin.
When they had spoiled it, they would watch for a moment
when Gertrude was not looking, and throw it out of the
window by the handful, until they found that she discovered
the trick when she weighed their work at night. Rudy's
children all declared at the outset that spinning was very
difficult, but Leonard's little Harry laughed at them, and
once, when his mother was not in the room, he bade one of
the others bind his eyes ; then, seating himself at the wheel,
he spun away as briskly as before. "We wouldn't have
believed it!" cried Rudy's children in astonishment.

"Oh, what you can't do blindfold, you can't do at all!"
remarked Master Harry.

"Learn to spin first with the use of your eyes," said
Gertrude laughing, as she entered the room and learned
what had transpired. And it was not long before all the
children, except the oldest girl, were completely accustomed
to the order which reigned in the mason's household.

Gertrude's kindness to Rudy was not limited to his children. Not a day passed that she did not go to his house
and see that everything about the premises was in order ; if
it was not, she took hold herself to remedy the defect, which
so put the good man to shame that he used to run about and
examine every nook and corner, before the hour of her
accustomed visit. Rudy also took more pains about his

clothes and person, and whitewashed his smoky little room, beside decorating it with prints of the Crucifixion, the Madonna and Child, St. Nepomuk, the Emperor Joseph II., the King of Prussia, and a black and white hussar, all of which he bought for the purpose at the village fair. Gertrude told the children they must not put their fingers on the beautiful pictures, else these would grow black. But this injunction was not pleasing to the little boys, and Master Rudy cried out: "There's somebody you can't forbid making them black!"

"Who is that?" asked his father.

"The flies. You know they made our mother's great cross and Jacob's Ladder so black that we couldn't read a word on them!"

CHAPTER XXIV.

WOMAN'S ARTIFICE AGAINST WOMAN.

THE more Gertrude visited Rudy, and occupied herself with his children, the more she became convinced that the present state of things could not last forever. "He must have another wife!" she exclaimed; and taking counsel with herself, she could think of no one in the village better fitted for him than the sister of the Bailiff Meyer. One day, while she was at Rudy's house, she chanced to see the object of her designs coming up the street, and running to the window, she called out good day to her. Meyer's sister returned the greeting, and asked: "Are you at home in that house?"

"For the present, but only till some better person takes my place. — But do come in, and see what good order Rudy's house is in."

Nothing loath, her friend sprang up stairs at a bound, and was filled with admiration at the new arrangement of the room. Gertrude led her out to the stable to see the beautiful cow which Arner had given Rudy. "I never saw a finer one!" exclaimed the unsuspecting visitor; and stroking the creature, she added: "It must be a pleasure to milk such a cow as that."

"Would *you* like to milk such a one?" asked Gertrude archly.

"Indeed I would!"

"But you have two fine ones at home" — and the mason's wife turned away to conceal a smile.

" They are nothing at all in comparison with this one,"
said her friend innocently, giving the cow a handful of
fodder.

Then Gertrude led the way past the long row of fruit-
trees, bending beneath their heavy burden, and over the
thickest grass of Rudy's beautiful meadow. Meyer's sister
praised everything, and presently asked where the children
were. " They, too, are quite different from what they were
once," said Gertrude ; " I will show them to you."

" And is their father, too, different? "

" That he is ! Why, you would hardly know him, with his
hair and beard and clothes all in order."

" That will be a good thing, if he ever wants to marry
again," said the visitor, still unsuspicious.

With this they went back into the house, whither the
children had just returned. Gertrude took little Rudy by
the hand, and smoothed back the golden curls which hung
down over the broad white forehead ; the boy leaned back
upon her arm, and gazed with great blue eyes at the stranger.
Nanny was a delicate child, but so beautiful with her deep-
set, flashing eyes, and raven hair fine and smooth as silk,
that the visitor exclaimed of her own accord : " This one is
an angel ! "

" And Lizzie will be a fine girl some day, I trust," said
Gertrude of the oldest.

" She hasn't so happy a face as the others," remarked her
friend ; and Gertrude gave the girl a significant look.

The children were all sitting at their new spinning-wheels,
and little Rudy placed himself with his behind the stove.
When the mason's wife called him out to show his yarn, he
was so elated at their praise that he sprang across the room
to the window, with a loud laugh of glee. "That is a wild
one ! " said Meyer's sister.

" Not so very," replied Gertrude, calling the child to her.

"Stand still, now; you know it makes dust in the room
when you jump about so."

"I forgot," said the boy, standing quiet as a lamb by her
side.

Then Gertrude went into the adjoining room, and returning with the baby, put it into her friend's arms. It had just
waked, and had the rosy flush of a healthy baby after sleep.
It rubbed its eyes and shook itself upon the arm of the
visitor, who caressed and played with it so lovingly that it
grew confiding, and reached after her mouth with its tiny
hand. She caught one small finger between her lips, which
amused the child, and when it succeeded in freeing itself, it
shook with laughter. In the midst of this frolic Gertrude
said: "If the poor little chick could only have another
mother!"

Like a flash Meyer's sister saw the game her friend had
been playing, and was vexed with herself for not having
discovered it sooner. She passed the baby back to Gertrude, saying she must go home immediately. "But don't
you think," persisted the mason's wife, "that these good
children are in need of a mother?"

"Who says they are not?"

"There are certainly no children in the village who need
one more."

"There I disagree with you. There are perhaps none in
the whole village who need a mother less."

"How can you joke about such a thing?" cried Gertrude.

"I am not joking in the least. *You* take the place of
seven mothers." And turning to the children, she asked:
"Tell me, now; wouldn't you rather have this kind woman
than a new mother?"

"That we would!" they shouted; "rather than a hundred new mothers!"

"You are making a stupid piece of work of it!" exclaimed Gertrude in vexation.

"*You* were trying to make too wise a one, I imagine."

"What do you mean?"

"As if you didn't know!"

"Well, I do think that in Rudy's present circumstances he can look for a wife where he will."

"Certainly no one will want to prevent him," observed Meyer's sister with a smile.

"You say that so sarcastically!"

"Shall I tell you why? It amuses me that you are such a partial advocate of his. You seem to fancy that any woman would stretch out both hands to be step-mother to seven children."

"I would like to find a *mother*, not a step-mother for them."

"Most women would think twice before taking such a step; seven children are always seven children."

"At least, most of them are good children."

"That may be."

"And he is goodness itself."

"I thought that was coming next!"

"It is true, at all events."

"And then I suppose he is a fine young man!"

"I didn't say so."

"It's a wonder you didn't!"

"But he does certainly appear younger"—

"Than he did six weeks ago."

"*You* have noticed it, then?"

"I think I must be going home," was the guest's only response.

"Just wait a moment!"

"Not a half a one!"

"But you really must not go away from the children without a friendly leave-taking," said Gertrude.

The other turned, and gave the desired salutation. "Did you hear?" she asked, laughing; "I said 'God be with you!' to them."

"And when you come again, you will say 'God greet you!'"

"When I come again, perhaps I will!" returned Meyer's sister, hastening out of the house. Her face was scarlet, and her step very different from that with which she had come. Gertrude followed her with her eyes, and felt that the first move in the game had not been without fair prospect of success.

CHAPTER XXV.

GERTRUDE'S METHOD OF INSTRUCTION.

IT was quite early in the morning when Arner, Glülphi and
the pastor went to the mason's cottage. The room was not
in order when they entered, for the family had just finished
breakfast, and the dirty plates and spoons still lay upon the
table. Gertrude was at first somewhat disconcerted, but the
visitors reässured her, saying kindly : "This is as it should
be ; it is impossible to clear the table before breakfast is
eaten !"

The children all helped wash the dishes, and then seated
themselves in their customary places before their work.
The gentlemen begged Gertrude to let everything go on as
usual, and after the first half hour, during which she was a
little embarrassed, all proceeded as if no stranger were
present. First the children sang their morning hymns, and
then Gertrude read a chapter of the Bible aloud, which they
repeated after her while they were spinning, rehearsing the
most instructive passages until they knew them by heart.
In the mean time, the oldest girl had been making the children's beds in the adjoining room, and the visitors noticed
through the open door that she silently repeated what the
others were reciting. When this task was completed, she
went into the garden and returned with vegetables for dinner, which she cleaned while repeating Bible-verses with the
rest.

It was something new for the children to see three gentlemen in the room, and they often looked up from their spin-

ning toward the corner where the strangers sat. Gertrude
noticed this, and said to them: "Seems to me you look
more at these gentlemen than at your yarn." But Harry
answered: "No, indeed! We are working hard, and you'll
have finer yarn to-day than usual."

Whenever Gertrude saw that anything was amiss with the
wheels or cotton, she rose from her work, and put it in
order. The smallest children, who were not old enough to
spin, picked over the cotton for carding, with a skill which
excited the admiration of the visitors.

Although Gertrude thus exerted herself to develop very
early the manual dexterity of her children, she was in no
haste for them to learn to read and write. But she took
pains to teach them early how to speak; for, as she said,
"of what use is it for a person to be able to read and write,
if he cannot speak? — since reading and writing are only an
artificial sort of speech." To this end she used to make the
children pronounce syllables after her in regular succession,
taking them from an old A-B-C book she had. This exercise
in correct and distinct articulation was, however, only a sub-
ordinate object in her whole scheme of education, which
embraced a true comprehension of life itself. Yet she never
adopted the tone of instructor toward her children; she did
not say to them: "Child, this is your head, your nose, your
hand, your finger;" or: "Where is your eye, your ear?" —
but instead, she would say: "Come here, child, I will wash
your little hands," "I will comb your hair," or: "I will cut
your finger-nails." Her verbal instruction seemed to vanish
in the spirit of her real activity, in which it always had its
source. The result of her system was that each child was
skilful, intelligent and active to the full extent that its age
and development allowed.

The instruction she gave them in the rudiments of arithmetic was intimately connected with the realities of life. She
taught them to count the number of steps from one end of

the room to the other, and two of the rows of five panes each, in one of the windows, gave her an opportunity to unfold the decimal relations of numbers. She also made them count their threads while spinning, and the number of turns on the reel, when they wound the yarn into skeins. Above all, in every occupation of life she taught them an accurate and intelligent observation of common objects and the forces of nature.

All that Gertrude's children knew, they knew so thoroughly that they were able to teach it to the younger ones; and this they often begged permission to do. On this day, while the visitors were present, Jonas sat with each arm around the neck of a smaller child, and made the little ones pronounce the syllables of the A-B-C book after him; while Lizzie placed herself with her wheel between two of the others, and while all three spun, taught them the words of a hymn with the utmost patience.

When the guests took their departure, they told Gertrude they would come again on the morrow. "Why?" she returned; "You will only see the same thing over again." But Glülphi said: "That is the best praise you could possibly give yourself." Gertrude blushed at this compliment, and stood confused when the gentlemen kindly pressed her hand in taking leave.

The three could not sufficiently admire what they had seen at the mason's house, and Glülphi was so overcome by the powerful impression made upon him, that he longed to be alone and seek counsel of his own thoughts. He hastened to his room, and as he crossed the threshold, the words broke from his lips: "*I* must be schoolmaster in Bonnal!" All night visions of Gertrude's schoolroom floated through his mind, and he only fell asleep toward morning. Before his eyes were fairly open, he murmured: "I will be schoolmaster!" — and hastened to Arner to acquaint him with his resolution.

CHAPTER XXVI.

MATCH-MAKING AND SCHOOL-MAKING.

ARNER rejoiced greatly over Glülphi's determination, and calling for the good pastor on their way, the two friends turned their steps for the second time to Gertrude's door. She had expected them, but had made no change in her usual programme. As they entered, at the close of the Bible reading, the morning sun shone brightly into the room, and the children, of their own accord, struck up the song beginning :

"With what a fair and radiant gleam
The sun's mild rays upon us beam,
Bringing refreshment to the eye,
And filling all our souls with joy!"

When they were all seated at their work, little Harry whispered in his mother's ear, to ask if the children might not thank Arner for the money he had given them, and on receiving permission, he noiselessly crept about between the wheels, bearing the message to his brothers and sisters. The little band came forth and stood shyly before the nobleman, no one daring to speak, until at a question from Arner, Harry plucked up courage to stammer out their errand. Arner lifted the boy kindly upon his knee, where he was soon as much at home as if it had been his own father.

Rudy's children now held a consultation, and came forward, black-eyed Nanny ahead, to thank their benefactor for the cow and the meadow. Arner set Harry down and took the little girl in his lap, where she was soon as much at her ease as the boy had been. In a minute she asked : "Have you much more of that beautiful money you gave the other children?"

"For shame!" cried all the rest in chorus.

"No, let her speak," said Arner. "Would you like some too?"

"Yes, if you please."

"But I have none with me at present."

"Don't you always have it with you?"

"No, but I shall have some when I come again."

During this scene it seemed to Gertrude as if somebody were urging her to say a word of her plan about Meyer's sister; yet her courage failed her when it came to the point of speaking. Just then the Bailiff Meyer happened to come in with a message to Arner, and as he was leaving, Gertrude forced herself to say, with a glance at the child in the nobleman's arms: "If the little chick could only have another mother!"

Arner replied that he should suppose it would not be difficult for Rudy to find a wife in his present circumstances. "Yes, but"— stammered Gertrude, — "but he ought to have a good one."

"Pick one out for him, then."

"I would be very glad to do so, if it lay in my power; but the Bailiff could do the most, if he would only have the kindness to say a good word to his sister for Rudy."

Meyer, who, with his wife, had far different plans in view, turned pale. "You hear what she says," remarked Arner to him. "What have you to say? Would you object to him as a brother-in-law?"

"Oh, — by no means," stammered the hypocritical Bailiff.

"Well, then, tell your sister that it would greatly rejoice me, if she would decide to enter this household."

"Oh, yes, Sir, yes indeed," answered the poor wretch, still pale as death.

"But you need not feel constrained to do this on my
account, if you have any objection," added Arner, suspecting that Meyer's inclinations were on the other side, and
wishing to leave him a loophole of escape. But he made
fresh assurances of his good will in the matter, and left the
house very ill at ease.

Glülphi had been waiting impatiently to speak to Gertrude
of his own plans, and he now asked her whether she thought
it would be possible to introduce into a regular school the
same method she pursued at home with her children. " I
am not sure," she replied ; " although I am inclined to think
that what is possible with ten children would be possible
with forty. But it would be difficult to find a schoolmaster
who would tolerate such an arrangement in his school."

"But supposing one could be found," said the lieutenant, " who would be willing to introduce it, would you help
him?"

" To be sure, — *if* one could be found," she returned with
a laugh.

"And if I were he?"

"Were *who* ?"

" The man who is ready to establish such a school as you
have in your room."

" You are no schoolmaster ! "

"But I will be."

" Yes, in some great city, perhaps, and in things village
people know nothing about ! "

" No, in a village, and in things all village people ought
to understand."

"That must be a queer sort of village, where a gentleman
like you wants to be schoolmaster ! Such a gentleman as
you doesn't take a fancy to teach children like these here."

" That you don't know."

" But I have an idea that it is so."

"So I perceive. But if I really wanted to be such a schoolmaster, what then? Would you help me?"

"To be sure," said Gertrude again, still under the impression he was joking; "I will help you all I can."

Glülphi turned to Arner and the pastor, saying: "You have heard, she has promised twice to help me."

"That's fine!" they said laughing.

Gertrude began to be confused, and when she found they were actually in earnest, she stoutly declared herself incapable of showing the lieutenant the least thing in the world, although she would gladly send her children to school to him, and come herself if she were only younger. But they answered that her help would be indispensable, and when she pleaded her lack of time and the cares of her household, and named another excellent housekeeper whose aid might be of service, Glülphi replied: "She will doubtless be useful, too, but there can be no substitute for your mother's heart, which I must have for my school."

"My mother's heart is hardly large enough for my own room," said Gertrude; "and if you are really to be our schoolmaster, I know you will bring a father's heart and a father's strength into the work, such as will make my little mother's heart quite superfluous."

"It is very true," remarked the other gentlemen, "that our lieutenant will bring a great father's heart with him; but that will not render the coöperation of your mother's heart unnecessary." Then they explained to her that they regarded the proper education of the youthful population as the only means of elevating the condition of the corrupt village; and full of emotion, Gertrude promised them she would do anything in her power to forward the good cause.

CHAPTER XXVII.

A SINGULAR COURTSHIP.

THE Bailiff Meyer hastened home with rage in his heart, having conceived the idea that his sister was in league with Gertrude, and had taken this method to further her designs. When, toward evening, he finally succeeded in finding his sister, he accosted her with an irritation for which she was at a loss to account, until he mentioned Gertrude's name. She turned very red, but he did not notice it, and proceeded to describe the interview at the mason's cottage. After a pause, she inquired : " What answer did you give them ? "

" You can readily imagine I had to promise them what they asked."

" That you would speak a good word for Rudy ? "

" I was obliged to."

" Indeed ? But how is it now ? What do you advise me ? "

" You surely do not ask me in earnest ! You know very well that my wife and I had other plans for you."

" I know ; it was only yesterday you were speaking of it. But then I cannot understand your promising Arner something different."

" Don't quarrel with me now ! I am in a sufficiently tight place already."

" You well may be, if that is the way you behave ! I wouldn't look a living being in the face, if I had acted as you have done ! " — and she ran off in great excitement to the mason's house.

Gertrude endured the passionate reproaches of her friend

in silence, until the latter had become somewhat calmer, and then volunteered to give her a true version of the affair. When Meyer's sister heard what feelings had actuated Gertrude, and learned that Arner had expressed the most friendly interest in Rudy's future wife and his whole household, her anger was turned against her brother alone, and her speech grew quiet. At this juncture Rudy came out from behind the door, where he had been an unintentional auditor of the conversation. When the visitor arrived, he was with Gertrude, and had followed her down stairs, with the intention of begging Meyer's sister not to be angry with Gertrude for her friendly intervention in his behalf; but, checked by the loud tones of the excited guest, he had drawn back and waited for an opportunity to address her.

Meyer's sister started back at Rudy's unexpected appearance, and measured her suitor from head to foot. Strange to say, as he stood before her, cap in hand, with a bearing which plainly showed that he had no hope, and was not there on his own account, — he pleased her so well that she stood still, and no longer scanned him with a critical eye. He, however, not noting this favorable change, begged her to pardon him for venturing to think of her, adding that he was in sore need of an excellent wife. She answered: " I can give you no hope."

He did not reply, but stood looking wistfully at her, like a hungry man who is yet loath to ask an alms. " Fie! " she cried; " you stand there like a beggar."

" I have never begged in my life, and yet I imagine that now I do stand before you as you say."

" But you should not! '

" How am I to stand before you, then, and what shall I do instead of begging?"

" You must pay no heed to me at all."

" Then I would rather go on begging."

" Well — then I must say 'God help you.' "

" If you will say that to me in the right way, I shall have no objection."

" Well, then — God help you, Rudy ! "

" Oh, that is not the right sort of ' God help you.' "

" What would you call the right sort?"

" If you would give me your hand on it, and promise *you* would help me, too, that would be the right sort of ' God help you.' "

" Indeed? You are certainly no fool, Rudy."

" Perhaps not; but, indeed, it would be hard to find anybody who has equal need of such an alms."

" But why should *I* be the one to give it to you? You can beg in this way at many houses."

" That I shall not do."

" Well, do as you please! Only now go behind the door again, and leave us alone." With this she took Gertrude's arm, and walked away, at a loss what to say next.

Gertrude praised Rudy and his household, and Meyer's sister took leave in a very different frame of mind from that in which she had come. Arrived at home, she seemed to see Rudy perpetually before her eyes, and hear his words in her ear. The rich cousin whom the Bailiff and his wife had intended for her husband also appeared to stand before her; first, as she saw him at his sister's wedding, eating bacon, with the fat dripping from the corners of his mouth ; and then, as she had seen him that other time in the village, when he was slaughtering a sow, and thrust his hand far into the animal's neck, until the warm blood gushed over it. She mentally contrasted the two men, and said to herself : "Yes, if I had to take one of them, it would certainly be the good old Rudy ; but it must be neither of the two."

CHAPTER XXVIII.

HOW SLANDER IS PUNISHED AND THE COMMON DIVIDED.

AFTER his visit to Gertrude's school, Arner sat down and
wrote a long letter to his intimate friend Bylifsky, now minister of the Duke, describing the impression made upon him
by what he had just seen, and stating the views of Cotton
Meyer with regard to the means of bettering the condition of
the corrupt village. "These views," he concluded, "can be
summed up under the following heads:

1 A school shall be organized which can be brought into
harmony with the developing influence of domestic life, as is
the case with that in Gertrude's house.

2. The better portion of the people of Bonnal shall unite
with the Castle and the parsonage, for the purpose of gaining a sure and active influence over the various households
of the village.

3. A new method of choosing the overseers shall be
adopted, whereby the evil influence exerted by bad overseers
may in future be removed."

It had been announced that on the following day the
apportionment of the common would be concluded. Arner
was setting out for the village in the morning, when he was
told that a peasant's daughter of the Eichenberger family
wished to speak with him. Arner had been overrun with
visits from the villagers ever since his kindly reception of
Gertrude, when she came to him in her trouble. He had
believed at first that it was his duty to grant a personal interview to any of his dependants who should see fit to seek him

at the Castle ; but lately he had come to the conclusion that
his time was being wasted in listening to much useless
gossip, while he was even forced sometimes to lend an ear to
falsehood and slander. A few days ago, he had resolved to
make an example of the first person who should abuse his
patience in this way ; and the opportunity now presented
itself.

He knew Eichenberger's daughter by reputation ; she was
one of those daughters of semi-rich peasants, who, through
the vanity and ignorance of their parents, are sent away to
third-rate boarding-houses in small towns, where they learn
to ape the customs and manners of city life. The maiden
in question had been still further led astray by her acquaint-
ance with Sylvia, an unscrupulous court *demoiselle* who was
related to Arner. Sylvia hated her cousin Arner, and was
particularly anxious to learn anything occurring to his discredit in Bonnal, that she might hold him up to ridicule in
the higher circles of society. With this laudable design, she
employed the above-mentioned peasant's daughter as her
newsmonger, allowing her vain informant the felicity of sitting by her side on the sofa during their confidential inter-
views.

Now Eichenberger's daughter had heard of Arner's
friendly behavior toward Gertrude and Cotton Meyer, and
imagined she might easily rise even higher than they in his
favor ; so adorning herself as if to attend a wedding, she
hired the best cart she could obtain, and drove to Arnheim.
Arner admitted her into his audience-chamber, and resolved
to let her speak uninterruptedly. She began in all confidence, lamenting the bad manners and morals of Bonnal,
and in her strictures sparing no one, not even Gertrude and
Cotton Meyer. Arner listened attentively, but remained
silent. By degrees this conduct confused her, so that she
began to contradict herself. But the more involved her

speech became, the more sharply Arner looked at her, still in this awful silence. She lost courage, and changing her tactics, modified and retracted her previous statements, until amid increasing embarrassment she hesitated and stopped.

Arner at length opened his lips and said: "Have you finished?" She could not speak, but gazed at him with fixed eyes and quivering lips. He rang, and his armed servant entered. Arner ordered the man to conduct her back to Bonnal in the eyes of all the world, so that another time she might have the wisdom to remain at home, instead of running to the Castle to slander the best people in the village.

Speechless with terror, she threw herself on her knees. It was fortunate for her that Arner's wife Theresa happened to pass the open door at this moment, and asked the meaning of the scene. When she learned the truth, she laughingly prevailed upon Arner to allow his suppliant to withdraw without an escort. Eichenberger's daughter did not wait for a second bidding, but flew home as fast as her feet would carry her, and wrote Sylvia a glowing account of the whole affair.

Arner proceeded to the village, where the people were assembled in the square under the linden-tree. After the lots were drawn, entitling the peasants to their respective shares in the common, he left the men to themselves, and stood watching them curiously. He remembered an old saying of his grandfather, that the distribution of property shows what people are, the possession of it makes them what they are. Every superior portion drew forth manifestations of avarice, which were exhibited in as many different ways as there were individuals. But this was only one side of the matter. Arner soon found that he could learn more of agriculture from these peasants, as they discussed the good and bad points of a piece of land, than he had ever

known before. The pleasantest thing of all was now and
then to see the delight of a poor man, when he had drawn
a good lot ; but the rich peasants wore discontented faces.

In the afternoon, Arner summoned the people again to the
common, and for a different purpose. A little before the
appointed time, a wagon loaded with several hundred fruit-
trees from Arner's own nursery-garden, moved from the parsonage, where it had been stationed awaiting his orders,
toward the linden-tree ; and at the same time a large herd of
goats was seen advancing in the same direction.

When Arner reached the green, he announced that every
father might go to the wagon, and take as many fruit-trees
as he had children. At this word the rich, the greedy and
the bold pressed forward to snatch the best for themselves.
But Arner ordered them to stand back, and wait until all the
trees should be taken from the wagon and laid upon the
ground ; then they might advance, one by one, and take
them in the order in which they lay.

After this was done, he called the people about him, and
said : " I am anxious that even the poorest household in the
village shall not be without milk for the young children, so I
have had these goats brought here, and will be glad to advance the money to those who are not able to buy one for
their children."

He begged those who would like such a loan, to come forward, and twenty-seven answered the summons. They were
hatless, shoeless and in rags, and worse than that, loafer,
fighter, gambler and drunkard was written on their faces.
Arner was heart-sick, and could not help exclaiming : " You
are a wretched-looking set indeed ! And the worst of it is,
that neither land nor milk will help you ! " He paused, then
in a moment continued : " If it were not for your children,
I would send the goats back where they came from. — But
go, in God's name, and pick them out ! "

The children whose fathers bought the goats were so over-joyed that many children of rich parents persuaded their fathers to buy them goats also, saying that Arner's little Karl had one. After warning the children not to form idle habits while herding their goats, Arner talked with the fathers about the tithe-free fields he wanted to promise to those spinners' children who would save up eight or ten florins from their earnings before their twentieth year. The wealthy peasants began to put their heads together, and murmur : " What will our own daughters have, if these spinners' children are to have tithe-free fields?" Arner heard it, and offered the same reward to any peasant's daughter whose parents should receive an orphan child into their house, and bring it up faithfully and well. But the rich men turned away grumbling.

CHAPTER XXIX.

A DAY OF JUDGMENT.

IT was the night before the day on which all accounts were to be settled between the former Bailiff Hummel and his debtors, and Arner could not sleep for thinking of the wretched crowd he would be compelled to face on the morrow. Little Karl, who slept in the room with him, heard him groan, and asked: " Is anything the matter, papa, that you can't sleep?"

" No, my dear boy," Arner replied.

"But, dear papa, I know something is the matter; you are anxious about to-morrow."

" How do you mean, my boy?"

" Papa, do you suppose I don't know that everybody is anxious about the reckoning to-morrow?"

" Who told you so?"

" Oh, a number of the boys; but one in particular. Just think, papa, he was with the other boys, but he hadn't the heart to play like the rest, so I went up to him, and asked him why he looked so sad. At first he wouldn't tell me, but I gave him no peace until at last he said that his family at home, his father and mother and sisters, were almost crying their eyes out, because they owed the Bailiff something; and to-morrow his sister must come to you under the linden. Then he began to cry so hard that he ran and hid behind a hedge, so that no one should see him."

" What is his name, and to what family does he belong?"

" His name is Jamie, and he is such a pretty boy!—so

good and gentle, too! You won't be hard on them to-mor
row, will you, papa?"

"I don't intend to be hard on anybody, but, my dear Karl,
you know as well as I do that when a bad habit is formed,
it must be broken up."

"Yes, papa. But if they don't do so any more, you'll be
good to them again?"

"I shall be only too glad," answered his father; and with
this word little Karl straightway fell asleep.

In obedience to the beadle's summons, by nine o'clock all
Hummel's debtors had gathered under the linden-tree, a sorry
assemblage of men, women and children, from the old toper
who had sat for the last twenty years at the Bailiff's table,
to the misguided child who a few weeks ago had entered
the tavern for the first time. As Arner sat with a sad face
beside the pastor, he suddenly remembered the conversation
of the previous night, and inquired about the family to which
Karl's friend belonged. The parson spoke of them in the
highest terms, as honest, industrious people. The wife had
been confined to her bed all winter, and her husband had
been obliged to watch with her night after night, without
proper nourishment, which had led him, from time to time,
to send for wine as a stimulant. His daughter, who had
brought the wine, had never touched a drop of it herself, but
insisted on coming to the linden in place of her father.

Arner's heart was filled with compassion for this unhappy
family, and for a while it seemed to him as if he could better
endure the sight before him. He pitied the children most,
and called them up first, to put them out of their misery.
He usually said only: "Are you there, too?" To some,
however, he gave his hand, saying: "Don t do so again, as
long as you live!"

Most of the women seemed ready to sink to the ground
with shame and terror; but he could see that the greater

part of this was put on, and treated them accordingly. When Lindenberger's daughter, Jamie's sister, was called, she did not raise her eyes from the ground, but silently laid the money on the table. Arner spoke kindly to her, saying he knew her history, and how she was not at all to blame, but had taken the disgrace upon herself to spare her father. The girl covered her overflowing eyes with her hand, as she sobbed out: "My father, nobody but my dear father can have told you this!"

"No," said Arner; "it was your brother Jamie who told it to my Karl, and he begged me with tears in his eyes not to be hard on you. Tell your brother, my girl, to come to the Castle on Sunday to see Karl; he is very fond of him." She sprang away home with tears of joy.

Others, who had witnessed Arner's kindness, tried to abuse it by exciting undeserved sympathy in their favor; but in vain. Finally the name of "Barbara" was called, and the poor spinning-woman answering to that appellation stepped forward. There was a movement of surprise among all present, of which Arner inquired the cause. The beadle, who was well aware of the truth, replied with a grin that they thought it was not the right Barbara. Hummel, being questioned, said that the Barbara who was in debt to him went by the name of "the pious," and that her pride had probably prevented her from coming to answer the summons in person. "And how much did she give you," inquired Arner of the other Barbara, "for coming in her place?"

"A half florin," she answered, adding that she had not thought it would do anybody any harm if she consented.

"But did you not think of its injuring your reputation to come before this table?"

"I thought nobody would believe it!" was the reply, to the amusement of all.

Arner sent his man-at-arms to bring the rightful Barbara,

whom he found solacing this bitter hour of affliction by reading the book of Job. All prayers and protestations were unavailing; the proud woman was obliged to accompany the soldier back to the linden, — if you wish to know *how*, good reader, you must recall to your mind the "Dance of Death" in Basle. Arner made the second Barbara sit down on the stone bench beside the first, and wait until all the other ne'er-do-weels had concluded their reckoning; then he called her before him, and simply said she must give her namesake another half florin for the service she had rendered, and another time must not try to purchase immunity from disgrace so cheaply.

CHAPTER XXX.

THIS same morning a portion of the village was very differently employed. The spinners' children had resolved on the previous day to form a procession and go to Arner, to thank him for his kindness. They rose bright and early, and devoted an unusual amount of time to the duties of the toilet, washing themselves zealously at brook and well, and allowing their tangled hair to be combed without a murmur. They put on the best clothes their homes afforded, which in many cases were only soiled rags, and gathered at the houses of Gertrude, Cotton Meyer's sister, and young Renold's wife. These three women, who had encouraged the children in their undertaking, borrowed shoes, stockings, dresses and wearing apparel of every sort, that the procession might be a pretty one.

When the whole band had finally assembled at Maria's house, she said: "We have forgotten to choose a queen for the procession, and teach her a speech to say to Arner." All three women looked the children over, and almost in one breath cried: "I know the one!" It proved they had all selected the same child, a poorly dressed girl, yet beautiful as the day, with golden hair rolling back from her fair forehead, and great blue eyes fixed upon the ground. She was standing a little apart from the others, absorbed in thought, and quite unconscious of the attention she excited. She was the oldest of the ten children of an unhappy man.

who, having fallen into Hummel's clutches, went into the woods one night, and hung himself. From that hour the child had never for a moment forgotten her father. During the day, she was the servant of her sick mother, and the mother of her younger brothers and sisters, performing every duty faithfully and uncomplainingly. But at midnight, when all the household were in their beds, a little figure would creep forth into the thicket to a lonely grave, which lay between rocks and lofty trees on the edge of a precipice. Round about it the child had planted the fairest wild flowers, — blue violets, pale greenish tulips, snowy anemones and delicate pink roses, with a great sunflower in the middle, and passion-flowers at the four corners. She had surrounded the grave with hedges woven of thorns, to keep off the wild beasts, and no human foot but hers ever visited the spot.

This was the girl who stood apart from the merry band, and did not even hear that she was chosen queen of the procession. When the children pressed around her, and rejoiced that she was to be their queen, her eyes filled with tears, for since her father's death she had lost faith in the kindness of her fellow-mortals. Renold's wife took her by the hand, saying: "Come, now, I will dress you like a bride, and teach you a speech."

The good woman attired her charge in a white dress of fine fabric, and was about to adorn her forehead with the shining band which the peasant-girls wear to weddings and baptisms, when the child drew back, and begged her to consider what Arner and the whole village would say if she should appear in such finery. "Let me answer for that!" Renold's wife replied; "you must wear it for Arner and the procession, not for your own sake."

The child submitted, and suffered herself to be placed at the head of the band with the passiveness of a lamb led by the shepherd's hand, and with as little personal vanity as might be displayed by a baby arrayed in cloth of gold, and placed upon a throne to be gazed at by an admiring multitude.

Arner had returned to the parsonage from the linden sick at heart, and almost discouraged at the idea of ever being able to elevate or improve a people which had sunk to such a depth of corruption. He walked up and down in the garden, a prey to gloomy thoughts, and at length seated himself in a dark arbor, which seemed to correspond to his frame of mind. Suddenly he was aroused from his musings by the sound of children's footsteps, and looking up, he beheld a youthful procession, extending throughout the entire garden, as if it had no end, and at its head, right before him, an angel in a snow-white robe, who thus addressed him:

"Dear Father Arner: we are the poor spinners' children of Bonnal, and have come to thank you for being so good to us, and promising us so great a gift if we lay up our earnings regularly. We also thank you heartily, because you are going to establish a school among us in which we shall be able to learn more than we ever had a chance to do before. All this makes us very happy, and we promise that while we are young, and when we grow old, we will do right, and show ourselves worthy of your benefits. May God requite you, in time and eternity, for what you do for us!"

The effect of this scene upon Arner was indescribable. He hardly knew for a moment whether he were dreaming or awake, and could not move hand or foot. Then he took the snowy angel by the hand, and asked: "Whose child are you?"

But his voice was hard, and his glance confused; his words also terrified the good child, who, pale and trembling, began: "My father" — but she could not go on, and covered her face with both hands.

" What is it?" asked Arner, almost as much startled as the girl herself. Another child that stood near, whispered : " She is the daughter of the unfortunate Rickenberger."

Arner was much grieved. He took her hand, and said : "I am sorry I asked you that. But it is to your credit that you are so fond of your father; I know he deserved your love, and was a good father to you."

With the little hand still in his, Arner gradually recovered from the first shock of surprise, and rejoiced at the coming of the children. The remembrance of their parents, who had stood before him that morning, faded from his mind, and he saw only the younger generation, for which hope arose in his soul. He felt himself the father of these little ones, and seating himself among them on the turf, he played with them as if they were indeed his children. The pastor's wife made a delicious milk-soup for the little company, and Arner's son Karl, as well as the parson and the lieutenant, came and enjoyed it with them. Their delight reached its height when Theresa arrived with the other children, and all sat together at the rustic banquet in joy and harmony.

CHAPTER XXXI.

THE ORGANIZATION OF A NEW SCHOOL.

GLÜLPHI was full of the idea of his school, and could speak of nothing else with Arner and the pastor. He used all his spare time in visiting Gertrude, in order to talk it over with her; but she seemed quite unable to explain her method in words, and usually deprecated the idea of her advice being necessary. Occasionally, however, she would let drop some significant remark which the lieutenant felt went to the root of the whole matter of education. For example, she said to him one day: "You should do for your children what their parents fail to do for them. The reading, writing and arithmetic are not, after all, what they most need; it is all well and good for them to learn something, but the really important thing is for them to *be* something, — for them to become what they are meant to be, and in becoming which they so often have no guidance or help at home."

Finally, the day arrived on which the new schoolmaster was to be formally presented to the village. Arner and the pastor led him solemnly between them to the church, which was crowded with the inhabitants of Bonnal. The good clergyman preached a sermon on the ideal function of the school in its relation to the home, and to the moral development of the community; after which Arner led Glülphi forward to the railing of the choir, and introducing him to the people, made a short but earnest plea in his behalf. The lieutenant was much affected, but mastered his emotion sufficiently to express in a few words his sense of the responsibility conferred upon him, and his hope that the parents would coöperate with him in his undertaking.

Arner was anxious to make the occasion of Glülphi's installation a festival for the school-children, so after the services at the church, he invited all the little folks to the parsonage, where, with the help of the pastor's wife, preparations had been made to receive them. It was a time-honored custom that every year, at Christmas and Easter, eggs and rolls should be distributed among the children of Bonnal. On this day, on entering the parsonage, the young people beheld even more beautifully painted eggs than they had seen at Easter; and beside each child's portion lay a bright nosegay.

The lieutenant, who knew nothing of the whole matter, was in an adjoining room, when suddenly the door was thrown open, and the children, at a sign from Theresa, struck up with one accord their prettiest song, and Glülphi found himself surrounded by the lively throng of his future charges. He was much moved, and when the song was concluded, he greeted them kindly, shaking many of them by the hand, and chatting pleasantly with them. Arner ordered some of his own wine to be brought, and the children drank the health of their new schoolmaster.

On the following morning the lieutenant began his school, and Gertrude helped him in the arrangement of it. They examined the children with regard to their previous studies, and seated those together who were equally advanced. First there were those who had not learned their letters, then those who could read separate words, and finally, those who already knew how to read. Beside reading, all were to learn writing and arithmetic, which previously had only been taught to the more wealthy, in private lessons.

At first Glülphi found it harder than he had expected;

but every day, as he gained in experience, his task became easier and more delightful. A good and capable woman, named Margaret, who came to take charge of the sewing, spinning etc., proved a most valuable and conscientious helper in the work. Whenever a child's hand or wheel stopped, she would step up and restore things to their former condition. If the children's hair was in disorder, she would braid it up while they studied and worked; if there was a hole in their clothes, she would take a needle and thread, and mend it; and she showed them how to fasten their shoes and stockings properly, beside many other things they did not understand.

The new master was anxious, above all, to accustom his charges to strict order, and thus lead them to the true wisdom of life. He began school punctually on the stroke of the clock, and did not allow any one to come in late. He also laid great stress on good habits and behavior. The children were obliged to come to school clean in person and apparel, and with their hair combed. While standing, sitting, writing and working, they always were taught to keep the body erect as a candle. Glülphi's schoolroom must be clean as a church, and he would not suffer a pane of glass to be missing from the window, or a nail to be driven crooked in the floor. Still less did he allow the children to throw the smallest thing upon the floor, or to eat while they were studying; and it was even arranged that in getting up and sitting down they should not hit against each other.

Before school began, the children came up to their teacher one by one, and said: "God be with you!" He looked them over from head to foot, so that they knew by his eye if anything was wrong. If this glance was not sufficient, he spoke to them, or sent a message to their parents. A child would not infrequently come home with the word: "The schoolmaster sends greeting, and wants to know whether you

have no needles and thread," or " whether water is dear,"
etc. At the close of school, those who had done well went
up to him first, and said : " God be with you !" He held
out his hand to each one, replying : " God be with you, my
dear child !" Then came those who had only done partly
well, and to these he merely said : " God be with you !"
without giving them his hand. Finally, those who had not
done well at all had to leave the room without even going to
him.

The lieutenant's punishments were designed to remedy the
faults for which they were inflicted. An idle scholar was
made to cut fire-wood, or to carry stones for the wall which
some of the older boys were constructing under the master's
charge ; a forgetful child was made school-messenger, and
for several days was obliged to take charge of all the teacher's business in the village. Disobedience and impertinence
he punished by not speaking publicly to the child in question
for a number of days, talking with him only in private, after
school. Wickedness and lying were punished with the rod,
and any child thus chastised was not allowed to play with
the others for a whole week ; his name was registered in a
special record-book of offences, from which it was not erased
until plain evidence of improvement was given. The schoolmaster was kind to the children while punishing them, talking with them more then than at any other time, and trying
to help them correct their faults.

CHAPTER XXXII.

A GOOD PASTOR AND SCHOOLMASTER; THE OPENING OF A NEW
ERA.

In his instruction, Glülphi constantly sought to lay the
foundation of that equanimity and repose which man can
possess in all circumstances of life, provided the hardships
of his lot have early become a second nature to him. The
success of this attempt soon convinced the pastor that all
verbal instruction, in so far as it aims at true human wisdom,
and at the highest goal of this wisdom, true religion, ought
to be subordinated to a constant training in practical domestic labor. The good man, at the same time, became aware
that a single word of the lieutenant's could accomplish more
than hours of his preaching. With true humility, he profited
by the superior wisdom of the schoolmaster, and remodelled
his method of religious instruction. He united his efforts to
those of Glülphi and Margaret, striving to lead the children,
without many words, to a quiet, industrious life, and thus to
lay the foundations of a silent worship of God and love of
humanity. To this end, he connected every word of his
brief religious teachings with their actual, every-day experi
ence, so that when he spoke of God and eternity, it seemed
to them as if he were speaking of father and mother, house
and home, in short, of the things with which they were most
familiar. He pointed out to them in their books the few
wise and pious passages which he still desired them to learn
by heart, and completely ignored all questions involving doctrinal differences. He no longer allowed the children to

learn any long prayers by rote, saying that this was contrary to the spirit of Christianity, and the express injunctions of their Saviour.

The lieutenant often declared that the pastor was quite unable to make a lasting impression on men, because he spoiled them by his kindness. Glülphi's own principles in regard to education were very strict, and were founded on an accurate knowledge of the world. He maintained that love was only useful in the education of men when in conjunction with fear; for they must learn to root out thorns and thistles, which they never do of their own accord, but only under compulsion, and in consequence of training.

He knew his children better in eight days than their parents did in eight years, and employed this knowledge to render deception difficult, and to keep their hearts open before his eyes. He cared for their heads as he did for their hearts, demanding that whatever entered them should be plain and clear as the silent moon in the sky. To insure this, he taught them to see and hear with accuracy, and cultivated their powers of attention. Above all, he sought to give them a thorough training in arithmetic; for he was convinced that arithmetic is the natural safeguard against error in the pursuit of truth.

Despite the children's rapid progress in their school, the lieutenant did not please everybody in the village, and a rumor soon spread abroad that he was too proud for a schoolmaster. It was in vain that the children contradicted this report; their parents only answered: "Even if he is good to you, he may be proud all the same." It was not until three weeks after the beginning of the school, that an event occurred which accomplished for him what the children's defence had been unable to do.

For the last twenty years the old rotten foot-bridge opposite the schoolhouse had been out of repair, so that in a rainy season the children must get wet above their ankles in

crossing the lane to school. The first time the road was in
this condition, Glülphi planted himself in the middle of the
street in all the rain, and as the children came, lifted them,
one after the other, across the brook. Now it happened that
some of the very persons who had complained most of the
lieutenant's pride, lived just across the way. It amused
them greatly to see him get wet through and through in his
red coat, and they fancied it would not be many minutes
before he would call to them for help. When, however, he
kept on patiently lifting the children over, until his hair and
clothes were dripping wet, they began to say behind the
window-panes: "He must be a good-natured fool, and we
were certainly mistaken; if he were proud, he would have
given it up long ago." Finally, they came out, and offered
to relieve him from his task, while he went home and dried
himself. But this was not all; when school was out that
day, the children found a foot-bridge built, over which they
could go home dry-shod. And from that day forth, not a
word more was heard of the schoolmaster's pride.

The school was still not without enemies, the bitterest
among them being the old schoolmaster, whose envy and
rage at its success would have known no bounds, had he not
feared to lose the pension which had been granted him by
Arner, on condition that he should not set himself against
the new order of things. But the schoolmaster was not the
only man in the village who looked back with regret to
bygone days. Half of the villagers had been accustomed
to spend their evenings at the tavern, and the bitterest
complaints were heard on all sides, because, after the affair
with Hummel, Arner had caused this house to be closed.
As soon as he learned the state of things, and found that
many of the former loafers were making their homes miserable by their idle discontent, Arner opened the peat swamps
in the vicinity of Bonnal, and at once supplied more than
fifty men with good employment.

The condition of the poor people of the village was much improved in various ways. The prospect of tithe free land brought order and thrift into the houses of many of the spinners, and the poor in general were no longer so servile in their obedience to the whims and exactions of the rich. Renold's wife, who had always been noted for her charity, began to see that more good could be done by leading the people to help themselves, than by all her alms-giving; and now, whenever her aid was asked, her first answer was: "I must go home with you, and see what you really need, and how I can best help you."

Every evening the lieutenant had a half dozen young people at his house, to whom he talked for hours of what Arner and the pastor intended, and showed how their designs had been misunderstood. Among his hearers was one young man, Lindenberger by name, who seemed to comprehend it all at a single word, and whose clear and forcible language served to set things in their true light before many of the villagers.

It was only the old generation, who were hardened in vice, for whom the new era that was opening contained no prospect of anything better. The quack doctor Treufaug, who had promised the parson to abstain from his evil practices, could not resolve to leave his old life and lead a good and useful one; the former Bailiff Hummel, when freed from the pressure which had been brought to bear upon him in the time of his great humiliation, and deprived of his daily intercourse with the pastor, fell back into his old ways, so far as his changed circumstances would allow; and Hartknopf, after a brief season of repentance, became the same canting hypocrite as ever.

CHAPTER XXXIII.

A DISTURBING ELEMENT AND AN EXCITING ADVENTURE.

ONE day Arner received a letter from his uncle, the General von Arnburg, announcing that he was coming, with his niece Sylvia, to visit his nephew for a few weeks. This Sylvia, who has already been mentioned in connection with Eichenberger's daughter as an enemy of Arner, had been brought up by the general's bounty after her father's death. She was headstrong and arrogant by nature, and these faults of disposition had not been corrected by her education, but merely covered with a veneer of social polish. She hated Arner, both for his philanthropic principles, and because he was heir to her uncle's property. In her ambition for wealth and distinction, she tried to induce Helidorus, the favorite minister of the Duke, to procure her a rich and titled husband as well as to influence the general to disinherit Arner in her interest. Helidorus was a deadly enemy to Bylifsky and Arner, as also to the schemes they advocated for the improvement of existing evils, and therefore was glad to make use of Sylvia's aid in obtaining information regarding the course things were taking in Bonnal under the new administration. He had been rendered very uneasy, both by the reports of Glülphi's school, and the news that Arner and Theresa, the pastor and his wife, Cotton Meyer and his sister, and the mason's wife Gertrude, met together every week to discuss the affairs of the village. Since, through Bylifsky's influence, the Duke was becoming interested in Arner's innovations, Helidorus felt there was need of a bold move on his own part, to nip the success of his rivals in the bud. It was accordingly with the hope of bringing Arner into ill repute, and making his dreams the laughter of the court, that he induced Sylvia to go to Arnheim, trusting to her known ability for mischief-making to take advantage of her opportunities when on the spot.

Arner was not without a foreboding of evil when he learned the projected visit; and indeed, Sylvia had not been many days in the house, before her influence began to make itself felt. She tried in every way to turn her uncle against Arner, talking of the unsuitable education he was giving his son Karl, and ridiculing the way in which he granted audience to every old peasant woman who came to the Castle. Worst of all, however, were Sylvia's attempts to injure the lieutenant. She caused the huntsman they had brought with them to spread various bad reports about Glülphi in the village, and the credulous peasants were not slow to believe that their new schoolmaster was a runaway soldier, who could find no asylum elsewhere. This slander was so injurious to the good cause in Bonnal, that the pastor at length found it necessary to inform Arner of the matter, and sent Michael with a letter to Arnheim.

It was a hot day, and there was company at the Castle. After drinking rather more freely than usual, the general had seated himself with Sylvia on the terrace. Suddenly she pointed to a peasant standing at the outer gate, and said: "Arner will leave us again now, as somebody has come for him." In the old man's excited state, this was like adding fuel to fire, and he called out to the fellow to be gone. But Michael would not depart without delivering his letter, and only drew back a little to bide his time. "There!" exclaimed Sylvia to her uncle; "you see, every peasant knows how much power you have here!"—and with such words she led him on, until he called to the huntsman below to chase the peasant away with the dogs.

At this moment, the general was summoned in to his game, and the huntsman would have calmly minded his own business, had not Sylvia beckoned to him to fulfil his orders. Karl was looking on, and when he saw the two dogs loosed and set on the unoffending man, he followed at full speed, calling them back. He seized Sultan, the hindermost, by the collar, and ran on with him, shouting : " Turk, Turk ! "

Sylvia stood watching the scene from the terrace, as if it were a comedy, and called after Karl. " You foolish boy ! He will not eat him ! " This was true ; indeed, the dog would not even have bitten him, had Michael understood his training ; for the dogs of the Castle were taught, when sent after poor people, to tear off a generous piece of their rags, and then let them go free. But Michael, ignorant of this, planted his back against the wall, and received the animal with his knotted stick, with the air of one who has seen dogs before, and is not afraid of them. Turk was so astonished at this unusual reception, that, forgetting his rules of breeding, he behaved like a dog without education, and buried his teeth in the peasant's thigh. Michael, however, being the stronger of the two, swung his stick, and dealt his assailant so sharp a blow on the ribs, that the creature retreated with a howl, just as Karl came up with Sultan.

" Come with me," said the boy kindly, reaching the wounded man his hand. Then he excused his father, saying that he was not at all to blame. " I know he is not," said Michael ; " and I would think none the less of him if I were to die of it."

" But you will not die ? — you will not ? " asked Karl anxiously, as he saw the red drops trickling down his side. The blood flowed more and more freely, and feeling he was on the point of fainting, Michael begged the boy to send Klaus to him as quickly as possible.

When he had done this, Karl went directly to the parlor,

just as he was, with rumpled hair and bloody hands, and pressed through the throng of gentlemen and ladies, to tell his father what had happened. Sylvia called out, with the cards in her hand, that she begged the young gentleman not to make such a fuss, for she had seen the whole affair, and knew that the fellow had gone away from the Castle safe and sound, so that he could not be much hurt, — besides, it was all his own fault. Arner interrupted her voluble speech, and requested her with dignity to allow the child to relate what had happened. The attention of all was aroused, as the boy began anew : " It is all *her* fault, — and nobody else is to blame ! "

At this moment the housekeeper rushed into the room, exclaiming breathlessly : " The man is lying dead on the lawn ! "

The words had hardly left her lips before Arner was out of the room and down the stairs, not heeding that in his haste his spur had caught in the table-cloth, dragging porcelain, glass and silver to the floor. Theresa followed him. As they reached the spot, Michael awoke from his swoon, and was much gratified by their sympathy. Arner himself helped him into the house, and causing his wound to be dressed with the utmost care, sent him home in a litter.

CHAPTER XXXIV.

THE PEASANTS TAKE JUSTICE INTO THEIR OWN HANDS.

WHEN Arner read the letter delivered to him by Michael, he groaned out: "It is too much for one day!" He trembled so with rage and grief that he could not finish reading, and Theresa, catching a glimpse of his face, exclaimed: "Good Heavens! You look worse than Michael himself!"

"I wish"— he answered with fixed eyes — "I wish that only a dog had bitten *me!* A worse beast is gnawing at my heart."

This sounded so unlike Arner that Theresa was terrified. "Do go to bed," she pleaded; "you are sick!" He was obliged to follow her advice, for when he attempted to rise, he sank back powerless. That evening he was in a high fever.

The effects of the wine over, the general, also, was unable to sleep that night. Confused pictures of the event with the dog filled his mind; he did not quite know whether he or Sylvia had been to blame, or whether the man was really dead. He heard Klaus going back and forth from Arner's room, and called to him to know what was the matter, and whether the man was dead. "No, he is not dead, but might have been; and my master is far from well," answered the servant.

The general questioned him narrowly with regard to the incident, and learned that everybody regarded Sylvia as the sole cause of the mishap. "Then many people know that she is to blame?" the old gentleman inquired.

" Certainly."

" And what did they say to it? "

" Your Grace can imagine what common people would say, when they think they might have been in his place."

" No, tell me just what they said."

" Well, then, they said it was a cursed trick, and it would be good enough for her if she should get her reward for it in this world. I beg your Grace not to be offended."

" Certainly not. God be praised that the man is not dead! "

" Your Grace may well say that on the lady's account."

" How so? "

" She wouldn't be sure of her life if he had died."

" But certainly no one would do her any injury now? "

" I wouldn't advise her to go very far from the Castle alone, Sir, until the first storm has blown over."

Encouraged by the friendliness of the general, Klaus went on to speak very frankly of Sylvia's unpopularity in the village, and also informed him of the reports she had been circulating about the lieutenant. The old man was overwhelmed by what he had heard, and going to Sylvia's room in the morning, he told her of Arner's illness, and reproached her for her conduct regarding Glülphi. Enraged at this reproof, she declared she had been slandered, and would go alone to Bonnal as soon as lunch, to investigate the matter. The general mentioned the warning he had received from Klaus, and besought her to take some one with her; but his very anxiety aroused her antagonism, and she set forth quite alone toward the village.

In the tavern by the wayside, that afternoon, the peasants were talking of Sylvia. There was but one voice among them; all declared that such an inhuman deed had not been done within the memory of man, and that it would be a praiseworthy action for the first of them who met her to set his dog on her. A butcher came forth from this conclave, and was driving his cart along the outskirts of the wood, when he saw a single figure on the road before him. Small, thin, dressed like no one else, full of all sorts of angles and flourishes, so that whoever looked at her saw something beside the individual herself, — yes, the description certainly corresponded, and the solitary wayfarer could be no other than the obnoxious Sylvia.

The butcher's blood seethed; his heart beat violently. He looked about him, but no one was in sight. He turned his cart into the border of the wood, while his strong young dog wagged his tail, and sprang to and fro. "Shall I, or shall I not?" the man asked himself. The temptation was too strong, and pointing with his finger through the fir-trees, he gave the animal a signal. The dog sprang forward, and in an instant had reached his goal. True to his training, he did not touch his victim with his teeth, but jumped upon her, sprang down and bounded about her, and then leaped upon her again, barking loudly the while. Sylvia's girdle broke beneath the paws of her assailant, and the thin upper garment tore from top to bottom whenever he touched her, so that she was soon surrounded by white fluttering shreds. The net from the back of her head hung down upon her neck, and its artificial contents fell out upon the ground, while the air around was rent with her screams.

The butcher calmly took out his watch, and said to himself: "Two minutes she shall have!" — at the end of which time he whistled the dog back again. The huntsman, whom the general, in his anxiety, had sent after his niece, heard cries of distress for some time, before it entered his head that such a screeching could proceed from the lips of his gracious mistress. When he came near enough to see the source of the disturbance, the picture which presented itself to his view was almost too much for his gravity, and he was obliged to turn away and compose his features, before he could come forward and ask the cause of Sylvia's sad plight.

To her explanation that a mad dog had assailed her, the huntsman lent an incredulous ear, and informed her that mad dogs were not in the habit of making rents in people's clothes without biting. Nevertheless, Sylvia was almost beside herself with fear, and fancied herself in the first stages of hydrophobia, although everybody assured her that the scratches she had received here and there were from the claws and not the teeth of the animal. She was also quite unable to give any description of the dog which had attacked her; it was larger than she herself, she said, — she had never seen such teeth, and such cavernous jaws. She could not even say what color the creature was, — it had appeared to her first white, then black; and it seemed to her now that she had seen nothing but its head and mouth. There was naturally nothing to be gathered from such an account, and nobody knew exactly what steps to take in the matter.

When Sylvia awoke the next morning to a calmer mood, she remembered to have heard a whistle from the woods, and had no doubt the dog must have been set on her. A desire of revenge at once filled her soul, and she advocated arresting every peasant who kept a dog and was in the habit of whistling. When her uncle did not favor such summary measures, she asked reproachfully : " Will you not imprison a single man on my account? "

" Not even a cat at random," replied the general coldly, as he left the room.

Sylvia's pride was deeply humbled, and she fell into a species of dejection. She felt of how little consequence she was in the world, and that she was not even able to carry out her designs against Arner. What no living man could have done, the butcher's dog had accomplished, — he had brought her to a knowledge of herself !

CHAPTER XXXV.

RESULTS OF ARNER'S ILLNESS, AND THE BETROTHAL OF A
STEP-MOTHER.

ARNER constantly grew sicker; each night the fever was
higher, and day after day saw his strength wane. Theresa
and the children could neither sleep nor eat from anxiety,
and every hour seemed a year. All the inhabitants of the
Castle were panic-stricken, the general most of all; he lost
flesh and color more than the sick man himself, and passed
more sleepless nights than he had ever done in all his life
before. The thought was ever present in his mind that
Arner must die, and he was to blame. Sylvia's condition
was scarcely better, although owing to a different cause, for
Arner's fate did not concern her in the least. The servants
were so incensed at the cause of their master's illness, that
a word would have sufficed to make them throw her out of
the window; and they would hardly suffer the huntsman
among them. Arner alone was calm, — for the fever had
left his head clear; and he spoke cheerfully with his wife
and friends of his approaching end.

When the news reached the village that Arner was at the
point of death, the children began to cry with one impulse,
and many of the parents wept with them, while all could
relate some kindness he had done them or theirs. But after
an hour had passed, the state of feeling was altered. They
regarded him as dead, and began to think what changes his
absence would bring about. More swiftly than the spider
spins its thread the strangest thoughts and desires were

evolved from the brains of these villagers. Whoever had wanted something which Arner had prevented him from obtaining, or whoever was not satisfied with the existing order of things, began to think : " Now all will be different."

The wealthy peasants had never forgotten the humiliation they had suffered under the linden-tree, and the paupers to whom Arner had advanced the money for goats, thought that now they would not be obliged to pay him. Wine was brought across the mountain to the tavern in broad daylight, and the herd-boys drove their animals into the enclosures of the poor, while the rich laughed.

The Bailiff Meyer had never felt so comfortable since he wore the mantle of office, and asked everybody from the Castle, with a melancholy face, whether it was really true that there was no hope of recovery. His wife was likewise content, for she thought her rich cousin, the innkeeper, might now be successful with her sister-in-law, who would certainly give up all thoughts of Hübel-Rudy. Meyer went to his sister to advise her on this point, but she indignantly repulsed him. It enraged her that they should imagine she could marry a man solely on Arner's account, and also that they should take advantage of the latter's sickness to deprive poor Rudy of his wished-for bride. " No ! " she cried, as soon as she was alone ; " I will show them that I don't take him for Arner's sake, but for his own ! The poor man has waited long enough, — I will take him now, in God's name."

Tears fell from her eyes ; she thought no more of either the Bailiff or his wife, and even forgot how she had come to her decision ; she only saw Rudy and his children before her, and their room with the engravings on the wall. Closing the door, she took down her prayer-book from its shelf, and read aloud the prayer of a daughter who is about to enter the estate of matrimony ; then laying her head upon her hands, she moistened the page with her tears, and prayed

God to bless her resolution. She finally dried her eyes, and
went with a full heart to the mason's house.

Gertrude was displeased with her friend for keeping Rudy
so long in suspense, and when she saw her coming slowly up
the street with an absent gaze, she had no suspicion of the
tidings she was bringing, and would not even step to the
door to meet her. Meyer's sister came in and sat heavily
down, gasping out as if short of breath: "I have made up
my mind, and am going to take him."

Gertrude thought she referred to the rich innkeeper, and
answered with sad reproach in her tones: "I wouldn't have
thought it of you!"

"What?" inquired her visitor surprised.

"That you could be such a weather-cock!"

"How do you mean? Don't you understand what I say?
Or what is the matter?"

"It grieves me that all of a sudden you turn round and
take the innkeeper, just because Arner is sick."

"Now at last you speak so that I can understand you!"
said Meyer's sister smiling.

"Can you laugh?" asked Gertrude with tears in her eyes.

"I have cause."

"Indeed you have not!—and you make me angry."

"Oh, I was only joking; he doesn't know it yet, and if
you will make it up with me, who knows what I might do to
please you?"

"You will drive me distracted!"

"And you amuse *me!* Don't you see that you are under
a mistake? I am not going to take the innkeeper"—

"But—surely you were not speaking of Rudy!" cried
Gertrude, a light breaking in upon her at last.

Soon after this explanation, the two friends set out for
Rudy's cottage. He was winding his children's yarn, but
the reel stood still in his hand when he saw them cross the

threshold. He could not move or speak. Meyer's sister seated herself beside him, and Gertrude said: "Now she is yours!"

The children rose from their wheels, and Gertrude said to them: "Now she is your mother!" Meyer's sister took them one after the other by the hand, saying: "Dear children, may God bless us together!" — and then Rudy, who held her hand in both of his, added: "God grant it!"

She spent the whole evening in the house, telling Gertrude it would give her pleasure to do as if she already belonged there. Accordingly, she took Rudy's reel, saying it did not go exactly right, and wound away merrily; she helped the children with their wheels, braided the hair of two of them, and cooked porridge for the little ones. She took the baby in her lap, and fed it; then undressing it, she held it a while naked in her arms, as the painted Madonna does the Christ-child; and after making it say good night to all its brothers and sisters, she put it to bed and sang it to sleep. When she went home, she picked a bunch of flowers from Rudy's garden, and carried it with her.

CHAPTER XXXVI.

SUSPENSE, JOY, AND A WEDDING.

THE idea became more and more diffused in the village that Arner's death would bring about a universal change. When the children came home from school and related that the lieutenant always had red eyes, many of the parents made answer. "He has good cause; his bread and butter are gone, when Arner dies." Speeches of this sort made the children so anxious, that after school they gathered about Glülphi, and the one who stood nearest asked him, trembling, to please tell them if he would not be able to be their schoolmaster any longer, in case Arner died? At first he was unable to speak, so much was he moved; he stood by the window and gasped for breath, like a man who is suffocating. Then turning, he stretched out both arms, and cried: "My children, even if it should please God not to restore Arner to us, I will still remain with you!" The children went joyfully home, but their parents did not believe his words.

When the village talk about the lieutenant came to Maria's ears, she begged her brother, Cotton Meyer, to insure the safety of the new school, and also induced the wife of the younger Renold to interest her husband in the project. They all went together to good old Renold, whom every one loved and respected, and he gladly consented to be their agent in the affair. He went from house to house, to all the richest peasants in Bonnal, and after laying the matter before them, remarked that if they were not willing to sign the pledge he carried, for the good of their children and of the village, he himself would stand surety for their portion of the expense of the school, and would write them down as recipients of this charity. This means was effectual, for no one was willing to be enrolled on the charity list; so that by evening the number of signatures was complete.

Meanwhile, the news of Arner's illness had spread to the court of the Duke, and Bylifsky begged for permission to set out at once for Arnheim. The Duke not only granted his request, but bade him take the court physician with him, and use means to secure Arner from annoyance of every kind. The renowned doctor shrugged his shoulders when he saw his patient; then he opened his medicine-box, and every sort of perfume filled the room. Frightful silver and gold pincers, needles, knives, sponges and bandages, pieces of snakes, pulverized flies, poison, metals, semi-metals, chemical secrets and natural powders, salves and plasters, all lay together in this chest. He weighed, mixed, rubbed, heated and cooled, and before an hour had passed, Arner had a sample of all the above on his body, and no less a variety within.

The condition of the sick man had become very critical; he fell into a sort of stupor. and the physician ordered the family to leave the room. They waited outside in terrible suspense, momentarily expecting the news of his death. Theresa had fainted; the children sank on their knees, and the pastor prayed aloud. Suddenly there was a slight movement inside; the doctor opened the door noiselessly, and whispered: "He perspires, and I still have some hope." A quarter of an hour later, the report was still favorable, and all through the suspense of that dreadful night the tidings were constantly encouraging.

The next morning he was decidedly better, but so weak

that the physician forbade any one to visit him. Bylifsky only saw him through the half-open door, and then spent the day with the pastor and lieutenant in Bonnal. The minister examined with the closest attention all the changes which had taken place of late in the village, and remained in the school during both sessions, from the opening to the close. He inspected narrowly the work of the children, and paid especial attention to the union of study and manual labor, but said not a word until he had seen all. Then he expressed to the somewhat anxious lieutenant the warmest approbation of his methods. "I find your plans in harmony both with the inner nature of man and his actual social condition," he said. "Man is only happy and secure in this world, when he is so developed as to be able to fill well that place in society to which he can legitimately lay claim. This demand is met by your methods in a more perfect degree than I have ever seen before. Yes, my dear lieutenant, if the Cabinet had wished to originate a plan by which the people should be educated from the stand-point of their greatest capacity for useful service, it would have been necessary to set to work in very much the same way that you have done."

A tear trembled in Glülphi's eye, but he could not speak. Bylifsky pressed his hand, and said in parting: "Count on me, but keep on with your work as if you did not know me, and as if there were no such person as I in the world."

Arner's recovery progressed slowly from day to day. The people of Bonnal now discovered that there was no one on earth so dear to them as he, and many were the tokens of sympathy and interest which he received. The children formed a procession, and went to the Castle to congratulate their beloved father on his recovery. He received them kindly, and talked long with them, of their school, their goats, and their savings. Before long, it was known in the village that the Bailiff Meyer had been replaced in office by Cotton Meyer, and great was the rejoicing of the poor at this event.

The first time that Arner was able to drive from the Castle to the Bonnal church, a grand festival was planned in his honor. The bells pealed at sunrise, and all the inhabitants, old and young, went forth to meet him. The children were adorned with flowers, and the procession was led by Rudy's bridal party, for he had determined to be married on that day.

When they heard Arner's carriage in the distance, they all ran to meet him, so that he heard their glad shouts of welcome before he could see them through the fir-trees. . He descended from his carriage, and hastened toward his devoted people on foot. After exchanging greetings with all, he placed himself at the head of the throng, with Rudy by his side, while Theresa led Meyer's sister, and the whole procession streamed joyously down the mountain to the church. There they knelt and gave thanks to God for sparing Arner's life, and sang a hymn of praise, after which the bridal pair was led to the altar.

Such a wedding had never been seen in Bonnal! The bells rang merrily, while Arner led the bride to the parsonage, and Theresa followed with Rudy. They found the house surrounded with chairs and tables, the latter laden with wine and bread, cheese and milk, sausages and cakes, enough for young and old. After this rustic banquet, the villagers danced on the green, being joined in the pastime by Arner and Theresa. Even the general and the pastor's wife danced too, and the hearts of all were full of joy.

CHAPTER XXXVII.

CONCLUSION.

OVER a year had passed since Arner's illness, and his beneficent activity flowed on unimpeded, with less and less friction as each day went by. He had supplemented his innovations with laws which should protect the interests of the individual, and at the same time impose a restraint upon every violation of order. The new Bailiff, meanwhile, took a step which astonished even Arner and the lieutenant. He assembled the whole community, and told them that, without any difficulty or hardship, they could collect within twenty-five years a capital sufficient to liquidate all taxes and duties which clung to their land like a perpetual rent, and thus transmit their estates tithe-free to their children. This he demonstrated to them could be easily accomplished by regularly laying aside a small proportion of each man's annual gains. Anybody who is acquainted with peasants knows that they would almost be willing to hang themselves for the sake of tithe-free lands, so it may be readily imagined that the villagers lent themselves with alacrity to the scheme, as soon as they were convinced of its practicability. Cotton Meyer also succeeded in convincing Arner and the lieutenant of the reasonableness of his views, and they saw plainly that a village which was in condition to amass a capital of forty thousand florins in twenty-five years could do far more, — that this would be but the beginning of its prosperity. The impulse which had already been given to economy and thrift in Bonnal had so greatly reduced the number of malefactors, that Arner now found it possible to remove the gallows, establishing in their stead a sort of hospital, in which the few criminals might be gently led back to better and more orderly lives.

In all this time, not a word had been heard from the Duke. Bylifsky was in constant correspondence with Arner, and showed the liveliest sympathy with all that went forward, but never referred to the Prince. This surprised and disturbed Arner a little, after the interest the Duke had expressed in their plans; but the lieutenant recalled Bylifsky's parting words, and felt sure he had good reasons for his silence on this point. He was right; the minister was so fearful that all would be ruined by a premature examination of the Bonnal projects, before they should become firmly enough established to guarantee their success, that far from trying to heighten the Duke's interest in Arner and Glülphi, he ceased to speak of them, and did not even oppose Helidorus when he ridiculed the philanthropic dreams of his friends before the court. Every one but Helidorus believed the whole affair was a failure; but the favorite was too shrewd not to see that the enemy had only withdrawn to strengthen himself for the battle which sooner or later must take place.

Arner was meanwhile in the greatest perplexity with regard to the general, who inundated him with letters, imploring him to cease making himself the laughing-stock of the court. One day he was sitting, trying in vain to concoct a satisfactory answer, when he was unexpectedly delivered from his dilemma. A letter arrived from the minister, declaring that the matter was now ripe for action, and that he himself was on the point of suggesting to the Duke to investigate the attempts which had been made in Bonnal, with a view to extending them more widely. Arner joyfully despatched this letter to his uncle, as the best answer it was in his power to give.

At about the same hour, Bylifsky asked the Duke for a private audience, and unfolded to him the progress of Arner's projects, calling his attention to the difference between the popular institutions of this little village and those of the realm at large, and drawing a vivid picture of the corruption of the land. " You know, Bylifsky," sighed the Prince, " how deeply I feel the truth of your words ; but I am quite convinced that it is impossible to improve the condition of things."

"Your Highness, I know it is difficult; yet I am convinced that there is one way, and only one, — and that is, for the government to exert an influence on the development of the people."

" Is such an influence possible?"

" The success with which Arner's endeavors have been crowned would seem to make it so."

" Can you see no difference between the government of a whole people, and the private influence exerted by a nobleman over his little village?"

"Certainly; but the means which Arner employed are just as much in the hands of your Highness, in respect to the country in general, as they were in Arner's with regard to his village."

" I wish you could demonstrate the truth of that statement."

" And would the names of Endorf and Nelkron be a sufficient guaranty?" asked the minister, mentioning the two men who stood respectively foremost in the state in finance and jurisprudence.

The Duke was thunderstruck on learning that two such patterns of caution and political wisdom favored the designs of Arner; but he exclaimed after an inward struggle : " No, even they shall not make me waste the last quarter of my life as I have the other three ! " Then changing his tone, he inquired : " What is it that you want? Money?"

" No."

" Strange ! What, then, do you desire ? "

" An investigation on the part of the state, as to the possibility of applying Arner's principles to universal government."

" And then what further ? "

" The establishment of a new professorship, for the purpose of acquainting the noblemen of the realm with better principles of popular government, and also the appointment of a commission, whose duty shall be to counsel and assist every one who shows a disposition to carry out these principles."

" Strange — very strange ! " mused the Prince. " And you need no money ? — no buildings ? — no institutions of any sort ? "

" Nothing but a few dozen account-books, in which to register all that is done by those connected with this commission, so as to have everything clear before one's eyes, like a merchant's debit and credit account."

The Duke meditated with himself a while, and then resolved to appoint a commission, under the control of Helidorus, to set forth the objections and difficulties in the way of a universal application of the scheme ; after which Bylifsky should have the privilege of replying to each point raised.

When the documents were placed in the Prince's hands, he marvelled at the weakness of Helidorus's side, and summoning Bylifsky, told him he had decided to investigate whether Arner had really accomplished all that was claimed for him, and if so, whether it were possible to extend his innovations to other villages, and so through the whole country. " And to insure thoroughness," added the Duke, " there must be among the examiners men skilled in law and finance, merchants, clergymen, government officials, schoolmasters and physicians, beside women of different ranks and conditions, who shall view the matter with their woman's eyes, and be sure that there is nothing visionary in the background."

He proposed to Helidorus to choose one department for himself in the investigation, but the favorite declined, preferring to watch the game from a distance. He only gave the Duke a parting bit of advice, as the latter was setting out for Bonnal. "These gentlemen," he said, "know that you are coming, and have wound up their clock so that it will go during your stay; but if you can manage to stop the principal wheels for awhile, you will perhaps be able to see the weakness of the whole machine."

The Prince had forbidden the examiners to express any opinion with regard to the several departments on which they were engaged, until they had reported to him; and this was a wise regulation. For at first sight, the whole affair seemed too ambitious, too exalted, for its universal application to lie within the power of man. Yet as they examined the details, day after day, they became more and more convinced of the practicability of the whole, and on the sixth day they unanimously recommended the introduction of the same principles into general government.

The Duke could hardly believe the evidence of his senses, when he found what had been accomplished by the simple application of human industry and wisdom   He talked with the lieutenant and Cotton Meyer; he saw the children of Hübel-Rudy, who had formerly lived in the depths of poverty and wretchedness; and Glülphi, pointing to Gertrude, said: " It was she who made them orderly and industrious, and she it was who had my school in her room, long before I ever thought of it; without hers, I never should have made mine what it is."

The Prince was deeply moved by all he saw and heard; he felt himself so carried away by his sympathy as to be no longer capable of a calm and disinterested judgment. At this moment he bethought himself of the advice of Helidorus. " I will be impartial, and will stop the wheels! " he exclaimed. Accordingly, he said to Arner, the lieutenant, the pastor and Cotton Meyer: "You must all four go to Sklavenheim, where I will leave you alone three days; during this period, examine the place, and find out how far you can apply your theories to the orphans and prisoners there. I will meanwhile try to take a calmer view of matters here, which seem to float before me as in a dream."

When they had gone, the Duke watched with the eyes of a lynx, to see whether he could detect any change in the affairs of Bonnal, but in vain; everything went its accustomed way, precisely as before. On the fourth day he set out for Sklavenheim, with no expectation of what awaited him. Under the lieutenant's charge he found a school like the one in Bonnal, begun with twelve orphan children; ten men from the House of Correction had, under Meyer's instruction, made rapid progress in the art of spinning; while Arner and the pastor had collected facts with reference to the history and treatment of the prisoners and the seventy orphans, which threw a hideous light on the present condition of popular institutions in the land.

While the Prince stood lost in wonder at the work of three days, he was aroused by a noise. The band of prisoners and the troop of children lay at his feet, and begged for fathers and guides like these four gentlemen. " Rise up, ye captives! " he cried; " rise up, my children! Your fate is in their hand." He could say no more. The children remained upon their knees, and a holy silence reigned, while all hearts were filled with sweetest promise for the future.

Printed in the United Kingdom
by Lightning Source UK Ltd.
102161UKS00001B/11